I0453406

Liberty Bell

Liberty Bell

Garrett Buhl Robinson

"Poet in the Park" and the "Solemn Swan" colophon are trademarks registered by Garrett Buhl Robinson with the United States Patent and Trademark Offices.

Library of Congress Control Number: 2025935199

Garrett Buhl Robinson © 2025
All Rights Reserved

Poet in the Park®
New York City
In Humanity I see Grace, Beauty and Dignity.
www.PoetinthePark.com

Table of Content

New Jersey Campaign

— 1777 —

New Jersey Campaign (continued)

Saratoga Campaign

Philadelphia Campaign

May ample justice be done them here, and may the choicest of heaven's favors, both here and hereafter, attend those who, under divine auspices, have secured innumerable blessings for others

George Washington

Proem

In the vast land of North America
    through decades of the 18th century
with nascent ideas of Enlightenment
    there was a tolling bell for liberty.

The English colonies had been sustained
    with their own means to satisfy their needs.
They raised their farms and generated trade
    supporting England's mainland industries.

The loyal British subjects had agreed
    to trade restrictions placed upon their ports
but Parliament abused the colonies
    by only levying excises more.

If Britain feared the possibility
    the colonies would gain their independence
the Crown and Lords and Commons should have seen
    the colonies were mostly self-sufficient.

It was not till the frontier war with France
    that Parliament sent British regulars.
The colonies had made their own defense
    with their own muskets, powder and reserves.

The colonies fought in the war with France
    and Britain had acquired more fertile land
but then the colonies were double taxed
    for victories the colonists help win.

The colonists accrued a wartime debt
    they paid collecting their own local tax
and then the people paid to Parliament
    more levied burdens strapped on people's backs.

But Parliament said colonies must pay
    for British forces offering defense
yet colonies could not defend their trade
    from being robbed by British Parliament.

The colonies had proved their benefit
    abundantly supplying raw resources
but as the mainland had been profiting
    the colonists' own profits were extorted.

The King said this was better for the whole
    and the well-being of all Englishmen
but Englishmen in colonies were told
    they could be taxed without their own consent.

They had a right for proper delegation
    in House of Commons in the Parliament
yet colonies were levied with taxation
    they could not legislatively contest.

Beyond the span of a whole century
    the Navigation Act restricted trade
and all the shipments of the colonies
    were taxed with duties from the high estates.

The colonies could only export goods
    for paltry sums exclusively to England
plus all the duties and excises took
    their profit from restricted sales to merchants.

The colonists were forced to buy the wares
    exclusively from English mainland works
and the inflated prices were unfair
    and stripped the means the colonists had earned.

The mainland wares were made with the supplies
    that the resourceful colonists had sent
and profit in the industries was high
    at the devoted colonists' expense.

The King claimed Parliament worked equally
    to serve the interests of all Englishmen
then why make taxes on the colonies
    that subjects of the mainland were exempt?

The colonists had raised productive farms,
    developed commerce at their own expense,
devised the local governments in charge
    and stood together for their own defense.

They weren't beholden to the British Crown.
    They weren't reliant upon Parliament.
They built the buildings of their settled towns.
    They were complete with their own management.

So colonists rejected the imports
    and lived in their own self-sufficiency.
They would sustain themselves in their accord
    to live complete and independently.

Then Parliament passed the Coercive Acts
    so colonists could not refuse imports
but colonists kept turning the ships back
    and said they would not shirk away from force.

Then one ship loaded from the West Indies
    was docked demanding duties to be paid
but colonists refused to buy the tea
    and dumped the bundles in the Boston Bay.

Then colonists said if they had no rights
    in the society of Englishmen
then they would independently reside
    and call themselves the free Americans.

1775

Chapter 1

Lexington
April 19, 1775

On April 19 shortly past midnight
   upon a road approaching Lexington
a horseman galloped through the bright moonlight
   with urgent news he carried from Boston.

Both Samuel Adams and John Hancock stayed
   at Reverend Jonas Clark's abode that night
as they were helping the militia train
   on open fields in the broad countryside.

In Boston Doctor Joseph Warren heard
   that Thomas Gage, the Royal Governor,
was sending British troops to seize and burn
   the powder Minutemen kept at Concord.

So Paul Revere and William Dawes were sent
   and they were knocking at the houses' doors
alerting all the local Minutemen
   the British troops were coming up in force.

Revere had stopped at Medford on the way
   and roused the residents to follow him
and found the house to certainly awake
   John Parker — Captain in the Minutemen.

Revere let both Hancock and Adams know
   the British planned to lock them up in jail
then haul them far away upon a boat
   to Canada or London for a trial.

The colonies had built judicial courts
    and practiced jury trials since Pilgrim days
but then the King demanded to enforce
    a feudal law with his pet magistrates.

With terms of royal charters compromised
    and colonists as vassals tending crops
the Bill of Rights of 1689
    and Magna Carta's Common Law were lost.

And as Revere was knocking at the doors
    the Patriots came walking down the road
as Lexington was stirring with reports
    the British troops were clamping down their hold.

With knocking, knocking on the houses' doors,
    the calling, calling of the Minutemen
John Parker soon arrived upon his horse
    to set about in organizing them.

The men had grabbed their muskets from their hearths
    that cooked their meals and warmed them from the cold.
They used the muskets hunting deer and birds
    but now they were defending their own homes.

John Parker then sent out a mounted scout
    to check the progress of the British troops
and set upon the Commons of the town
    to check the British force from marching through.

Some of the men had fought against the French
    but most of them were common, country folk
who drilled together for their homes' defense
    aside from their own daily chores and toils.

They were secure freeholders of their land.
    They were not vassals of a feudal lord.
They were entitled rights of Englishmen
    that Crown and Parliament seemed to ignore.

A year before the British army came
    but did not set in Boston to protect.
The King was pressing with his sovereign reign
    asserting his divine will to oppress.

The colonists defended their own land.
    They did not call upon the sovereign Crown.
They did not ask for aid from the mainland.
    They managed for themselves upon their own.

The colonists built their own equity
    in the development of the new world
and organized their own communities
    — constructing and maintaining civil works.

They built their local schools and colleges
    with eagerness to learn and understand,
communicating through the printing press
    to freely speak and praise the Rights of Man.

The colonists were not just corporations
    to boost the profits for the King's empire.
The colonies were of the British kingdom
    and colonists demanded Common Rights.

And then the King appointed Governors
    against the interests of the colonies
and then appointed judges in their courts
    enforcing Parliament's severities.

The colonists shipped the materials
    supplying English manufacturing
for what the colonists could make themselves
    as they developed their own industry.

They did not lack any ability.
    They were prohibited by Parliament.
They had abundant ingenuity
    and were not lacking in initiative.

There was no justice blocking their demands
    when their demands were for their Common Rights
yet they were forced into subservience
    and being pressed they were prepared to fight.

The mounted scout returned before twilight
    with the report of what he heard and saw.
The British force was marching through the night
    and the advance would soon arrive at dawn.

The total force was 700 men,
    a full brigade of British infantry.
200 men were marching in advance
    in grenadier and shock troop companies.

Then Captain Parker mustered up the men.
    The drummer sounded off the call to arms
and they were set for a line of defense
    to face the British on their forward march.

The men stood with their muskets at their chests
    with 70 New Englanders in line
and Parker paced before the Minutemen
    and light had just begun to touch the sky.

And Parker knew what they were up against.
    The redcoat force was marching to the drum.
And Parker paced the line of the brave men
    and regulars would soon be coming up.

Their boots were wet with early morning dew
    and faintly they could hear the tapping drum
and although not yet coming into view
    the British regulars were coming up.

Then Captain Parker drew his polished sword
    and faced the men defending liberty
and with the careful weighing of his words
    gave them the orders for all history.

"Stand your ground. Don't fire unless fired upon."
    Then said, "But if they mean to have a war"
and paused for a clear moment in the dawn
    and said out loud, "then let it begin here."

Then in their files the British came in sight
    and the commander saw the Minutemen
and steered the regulars to form a line
    in a position to face the defense.

The companies unfolded with the drill
    and pivoted in step with cadenced march,
outstretching orderly upon the field
    and snapped together with the call to arms.

A wall of scarlet coats stood three rows deep
    and moved together as a war machine
and the commander sat upon his steed
    beside the firing line of infantry.

"By order of the royal British King"
    the stern commander began to announce,
"defiant contests of the sovereignty
    will promptly and severely be put down.

"By order of the scepter, crown and throne
    before the peace is terribly disturbed
disband and promptly go back to your homes.
    Put down your arms and biddably disperse!"

The field grew brighter with the rising sun.
    The hearts were pounding in the chests of men
but all the Patriots stuck to their guns
    and held their muskets firmly in their grips.

Then one man shouted proud and strong and bold,
    "We own this land. We built our homes and farms.
We built our church and town and cleared the roads.
    We will not yield. We will not drop our arms."

Then the commander ordered bayonets
    and there was the metallic clicking sound
as redcoats busied in attaching them.
    And Captain Parker ordered, "Stand your ground."

Then after bayonets had been attached
    the stern commander reigned his restless horse
and shouted out to threaten an attack,
    "Disperse or ye will swiftly be destroyed!"

The Patriots stood firmly in their place
    then the commander once again called out,
"Disperse ye villains! Move out of the way!"
    but the stout Patriots would not back down.

Then suddenly a single shot rang clear
    and Parker looked down the long line of men.
There was no smoke that he saw anywhere
    as all his men were standing as they'd been.

Then Parker turned to look at the redcoats
    to search for signs of who had made the shot
but there was not a single wisp of smoke
    and not a single soldier's gun was hot.

But then the redcoats lifted up their guns
    while looking down their barrels for their aim
and instantly the tension had been sprung
    as Parker saw a solid wall of flame.

That instant bullets whistled through the breeze
    — the tiny bees that buzz with deadly stings
by punching in the body violently
    and several men collapsed upon the green.

The Minutemen then lifted up their guns
    but fired before the clouds of smoke were cleared
and then the regulars charged in a run
    and through the smoke the bayonets appeared.

The line of Minutemen were overwhelmed,
    reloading, some were stabbed by bayonets
and in the rushing moment brave men fell
    and British soldiers stood over the dead.

The others backed away in a withdrawal
    and kept their guard from where the British stood
and helped the injured soldiers who could walk
    to look for cover in surrounding woods.

Chapter 2

Concord
April 19, 1775

In Concord Minutemen had been forewarned
  and they were busy hiding powder kegs
and diligently through the early morn
  they moved the powder where it could be hid.

The British had restricted colonies
  from building up their strength with armaments
and so gunpowder was a scarcity
  that Patriots would need for their defense.

In Lexington the British had reformed.
  The avant-garde was joined by the brigade
and 700 British regulars
  were marching onto Concord that same day.

And on the roads from the surrounding farms
  the Minutemen were answering the call
with powder horns and duck guns in their arms
  for liberty and justice for them all.

By 10 AM the British had arrived
  and searched the homes of local families
and rolled some barrels through the doors outside
  to smash them in the middle of the street.

But they were disappointed when they found
  the barrels were not filled with black gunpowder
but staples of the quaint New England town
  with millstone grindings of the farmers' flour.

Then soldiers stormed into the shops and sheds
    and rolled out carriages and wagon wheels
and then set fire to burn the carriages
    as if they were supplies for battlefields.

Then while the soldiers searched inside the homes
    the British sent some companies to post
on routes where the militia might approach
    upon the bridges of the country roads.

Three companies marched to the British right
    to block a bridge that was three miles away.
The sun continued rising in the sky
    and would soon reach the zenith of the day.

Along a road the Minutemen had gathered
    to organize for mounting an offense
and they stood by the gentle flow of water
    where town folk had constructed the North Bridge.

They knew the British marched for an attack
    and men were coming in from all around
and they expected their homes were ransacked
    by British regulars inside their town.

The Minutemen were building up their force
    and many others had not yet arrived.
They needed every soldier to report
    to face the British army in a fight.

Then at high noon they heard the marching drum
    as the redcoats were coming up the road
and Minutemen were reaching for their guns
    and with the ramrods tamping down their loads.

Then the commanders ordered Minutemen
    to line along the Concord River shore
as British soldiers were approaching them
    in one long column marching in strict form.

The drums were tautly tapping marching steps
    as regulars continued to approach.
The heavy boots were stomping in cadence
    with rows and rows of muskets and redcoats.

Across the river standing at the bridge
    the Minutemen were guarding the roadway.
The sun was high, directly overhead
    with British soldiers marching into range.

Then off in the direction of the town
    they saw the smoke that rose into the sky
and seeing that their homes were burning down
    the Patriots began to open fire.

And all along the Concord River side
    the muzzles flashed as musket balls were hurled.
Then British soldiers tried to form a line
    so they could send a volley in return.

The British soldiers tried to wheel around,
    maneuvering while harried with attack
and Minutemen were tamping more loads down
    and pouring in the bullets without slack.

The British companies became confused
    although some soldiers got a few shots off
and yelling to reorganize the troops
    the officers then ordered a withdrawal.

As British regulars were turning back
    the Minutemen came running cross the bridge
as lumbered boards were thrumming with their tracks
    and then they set to load their guns again.

The British then were marching back in town
    and Minutemen were keeping them in range.
The redcoats could not stop to turn around
    but then they were rejoined by the brigade.

Then outside Concord on the country way
    the Patriots' pursuit abruptly stopped
when they ran straight into a whole brigade
    that was lined up to fire a volleyed shot.

The Minutemen then turned and ducked for cover
    and suddenly there was a thundered roar
as hundreds of the British ranks of soldiers
    sent bullets flying by the countless scores.

The trees were raining leaves like it was autumn
    as bullets cut the stems from limb to limb
and then the British soldiers were reloading
    to send a fiery volley once again.

The King's brigade was standing in the open
    with the commander's regimented call
while centering upon a roadway crossing
    surrounded by the woods and stonework walls.

Then something happened that was quite astounding,
    the meadow walls appeared to come alive
as muzzles were extending from the cover
    and then from all directions opened fire.

The British recognized they were surrounded
    as Minutemen from all the countryside
had seen the smoke and heard the shots resounding
    and rushed to Concord to join in the fight.

The regulars were turning every way
    and spinning round in circles here and there.
They could not find a mark to set their aim.
    The musket balls were flying everywhere.

The British still outnumbered Minutemen
    but they could not form in a firing line
and the commander sent the order in
    and drummers beat retreat at double time.

But as the regulars marched down the road
    the Minutemen were lined up on the sides
and just as quickly as they could reload
    they harried regulars with galling fire.

The rear guard tried to cover the retreat
    but Minutemen kept sprouting one by one
as a spring harvest had been ripening
    and then a revolution had begun.

The British soon returned to Lexington
    and General Percy had brought reinforcements.
The two brigades of regulars then formed
    to face the Patriots who were approaching.

The British found the high ground east of town
    then set the soldiers to defend the spot
and loaded cannons with the iron rounds
    and cleared the road with blasts of 6 pound shot.

The Patriots continued the pursuit
   but there were 1500 regulars
and a direct attack would surely lose
   so they surrounded the perimeter.

The British then continued their withdrawal
   and every mile more Minutemen arrived
and there were guns at every tree and wall
   as the whole countryside had come alive.

The British had to march 16 long miles
   with paces often peppered to a run.
The Minutemen did not let up their fire
   until they were outside of Charlestown.

The Minutemen stopped there to spare the town.
   They did not want to fire into their homes
and the long route they chased the British down
   will always be known as the Battle Road.

Chapter 3

Travelling News
April – June, 1775

The news from Massachusetts travelled round
    with printing presses in the colonies
distributing reports from town to town
    with the prospects of gaining liberty.

Debates had been conducted many years
    with pamphlets that outlined the arguments.
The people of the colonies had cared
    about the policies effecting them.

The colonists enjoyed their independence
    yet still considered themselves Englishmen.
They were affirmed by living self-sufficient
    for the well-being of the common man.

They did not trouble of the sceptered King
    with what they could accomplish on their own.
The Lords and King could tend their majesties.
    The colonists could manage their own homes.

They raised their farms to harvest their own food
    and with their harvests they developed trade
and their prosperity for common good
    was benefiting British heritage.

And as the colonists built in success
    they were the mainland's major customers,
assuring everyone was prosperous
    by buying English manufactured wares.

But Parliament persisted with restraints
   for royal shipments sent across the sea.
At first it was for regulating trade
   but then they were excising everything.

The more the English colonies excelled,
   the more was taken from their property.
How could they try promoting common wealth
   when Parliament promoted poverty?

The colonists had ventured for the good.
   They did not burden. They were diligent.
The soundness of their effort firmly stood
   yet they were punished for their own success.

Ben Franklin had proposed decades before
   a unity between the colonies
but both the King and Parliament were floored
   — the colonies would then gain too much strength.

How could the colonists be Englishmen
   with Common Rights the Magna Carta states
if Crown and Lords and Commons punished them
   for their enrichment of the King's domain?

These were not trifles colonists discussed.
   These were the matters of their livelihoods
and the legalities were ponderous
   for what was truly for the common good.

Men gathered round the Massachusetts Bay,
   assembling from the other colonies,
and the militia swelled with numbered ranks
   with answers to the call of liberty.

They heard the calling for a revolution
    in both New Hampshire and Connecticut.
The men marched in from western Massachusetts
    and then Rhode Island men were stepping up.

The strong and rugged Patriots converged,
    at least 10,000 shouldering their arms
and Thomas Gage, the royal Governor,
    was fortifying Boston in alarm.

In May the Continental Congress met
    more centrally in Philadelphia
and colonies sent representatives
    to Franklin's town in Pennsylvania.

The leaders of the colonies agreed
    events of consequence were underway
and their sole hope for reaching victory
    was only if they could cooperate.

Mid-June they set a budget commonly
    and formed the Army of the Continent
with troops they'd mustered from the colonies
    under command of General Washington.

And Washington accepted the appointment
    but said that he would not accept a wage.
He answered for his duty, not for profit.
    Their liberty was all he hoped to gain.

Chapter 4

Bunker Hill: Digging In
June 16 – 17, 1775

Before George Washington was riding north
    the Patriots had set the Boston siege
and pinned down British forces at the port
    where they had only access to the sea.

The Patriots controlled the countryside
    but British forces occupied their town.
The British were cut off from more supplies
    but could live comfortably in Boston homes.

Of course the colonists had built those homes.
    They stockpiled the provisions in the stores
but Parliament wrote acts so they were forced
    to feed and quarter British men of arms.

On June 16 the setting would soon change
    and soldiers craved for some activity.
The situation was in a stalemate
    and they demanded that the British leave.

One of the soldiers, Doctor Joseph Warren
    was contemplating the predicament.
He met with the commanders in the morning
    and they discussed the plans that had been set.

The Patriots had need for higher ground
    to mount artillery upon the bay
and threatening to cannonade the town
    they'd force the British to evacuate.

Joe Warren had a very humble youth,
    a barefoot milk boy running to the market
but while in school he proved to be astute
    and was admitted into Harvard College.

He worked to comfort lives with medicine
    but then he needed to become a soldier.
Both lines appeared to point to different ends
    yet still both lines were for the sake of others.

He had become a man of prominence
    as President of the Provincial Congress.
He was one of the leading Patriots
    yet modestly enlisted as a private.

Despite success the Doctor stayed quite humble
    yet was appointed as the army surgeon
and given the commission as a General
    to shoulder heavy weights of duty's burden.

Across Back Bay he saw the precious city
    that generations built with their own hands
and pausing he admired the quiet beauty
    where rows of homes were lined upon the land.

To clear the enemy from their own town,
    must they fire cannon shot at their own homes?
Must everything they've done come tumbling down
    before their independence could be won?

But what can people claim and hope to have
    if those same people cannot say they're free?
Life has no meaning if the people lack
    the right to live their lives in liberty.

When Parliament can arbitrarily
    demand that soldiers occupy their homes
and toss all their belongings in the streets
    how can they claim those homes to be their own?

The British were not offering defense.
    They'd closed the harbor down for the past year
and blocked the trade and shipments coming in,
    intimidating with suppressive fear.

But the New England Patriots had shown
    that they were not afraid of bully threats
and if they had to sacrifice their homes
    they would be free to build them up again.

At 6 PM the troops were notified
    to pack one day's provisions and bed rolls
and they began to march in the twilight
    with muskets, shot and the entrenchment tools.

1200 men then marched clandestinely
    to the peninsula of Charlestown
to dig a redoubt for a battery
    and drop the shot on British from above.

With Boston within easy cannon range
    the British would be forced to fight or flee
and as the British had to cross the bay
    the Patriots could set defensively.

They crossed the neck and over Bunker Hill
    then marched directly to Breed's Hill nearby
and Colonel William Prescott marked with skill
    dimensions of the fortified design.

Then on the stark and barren little knoll
    with picks that swung and sunk in with a thump
while prying loose the dirt of rocky soil
    the shovels started rasping as they dug.

Through the whole summer night the soldiers worked
    and slowly the redoubt came into shape
while digging down and piling up the earth
    for battlements to fortify the place.

Then Prescott noticed how the rocky knoll
    could be surrounded to block a retreat
— the line's left flank was open and exposed,
    and ordered trenches dug down to the beach.

Along the beach instead of digging sand
    the soldiers built a barrier with rocks
and men set rails of fences on the land
    preparing for the infantry's assault.

Before at Concord, Patriots had won
    with a triumphant day of victory
while harrying the British on the run
    when they could not reform their infantry.

But this time they would have to hold position
    and they would feel the brunt of British strength.
Bill Prescott knew the force would be relentless
    and they must be prepared defensively.

The cannons of the redoubt had come up
    and they had brought the rounds of 6 pound shot
but they would be surrounded by gunships
    with a barrage of British shells and bombs.

Most Patriots had not yet seen combat
   and there would be long lines of regulars.
This would not be a tussle or contest.
   This day they would experience a war.

When early rays of light had touched the clouds
   the watches on the gunships were alert
and saw the earthwork of the fresh redoubt
   and roused the British sailors from their berths.

The sailors tossed the kedges overboard
   and heaved the lines to turn the ships' broadsides
then rows of muzzles nudged through the port doors
   and thunder rolled as they began to fire.

The 17th of June was underway.
   The redoubt on the hill was taking shape.
Then gunners on the ships were finding range
   and kept up with a steady cannonade.

The British sent a flurry of their shot
   and cannon balls were screaming through the air
and the redoubt upon the rounded top
   was taking fire that came from everywhere.

The gunships and the floating batteries
   were joined with Copp's Hill ground artillery
and all the British guns on land and sea
   were pounding on Breed's Hill relentlessly.

There was more work that needed to be done
   to strengthen the redoubt upon Breed's Hill
but the raw troops sought cover from the guns
   and Prescott had to spirit them to build.

So Colonel Prescott climbed on top the wall
    where solid shot and bombs were flying thick
and with his dauntless voice began to call
    the Patriots to grab their tools and dig.

"The British will be marching up this hill
    and we must be prepared for our defense.
The preparations needed on the field
    must be complete before assaults begin."

While Prescott bravely stood upon the berm
    the Patriots were looking up at him
and he began to point out needed work
    ensuring that they had a strong defense.

He ordered more entrenchments on the knoll
    to bulwark the blind side of the north slope
so when the battle started to unfold
    they'd cover every possible approach.

Then Prescott recognized they'd need more men.
    The line down to the beach had gaps wide open.
He knew the British would show all their strength
    and sent someone to call for reinforcements.

The soldiers worked to build and fortify
    and British cannons kept up the attack.
Then Patriots began returning fire
    but four 6 pounders hardly were a match.

Then peering cross the waters of the bay
    Bill Prescott saw the redcoats at the wharf.
The garrison was lined up for the day
    and marched to load on infantry transports.

They needed to make sure they were well set.
    Their fortified defenses must be made.
When British forces reached the hilltop's edge
    if they weren't ready, it would be too late.

The men were willing to put in the fight
    and Colonel Prescott needed to make sure
when they went up against the British lines
    the strength in the position was secure.

Then Prescott kept his eye upon the wharf
    to watch where British transports planned to go
and see where on the shore they'd disembark
    and then from which direction they'd approach.

And Prescott ordered gunners of the cannons
    to aim upon the infantry transports
and try to do whatever kind of damage
    to rattle and disturb the British nerves.

The ships continued with the cannonade.
    The British had abundant war supplies.
And Colonel Prescott saw his men display
    their growing steadiness while under fire.

Most of the shot was flying overhead
    but they were hit with several casualties
and Doctor Warren turned to help attend
    the Patriots who suffered injuries.

After the transports loaded at the wharf
    they sailed into the open of the bay
as the 2000 British regulars
    had been deployed for battle on that day.

Then as the surge of tide was coming in
    the British set their aim upon the shore
to land on the peninsula's east end
    and disembarked the troops at Moulton Point.

The British landed shortly after noon
    and they were less than half a mile away.
Bill Prescott watched them organize their troops
    and set the ranks of soldiers in array.

Then Prescott sent some soldiers to the right
    to set in Charlestown clandestinely
so if the British came across that side
    the marksmen could attack them from the streets.

Some soldiers noticed a calm peacefulness
    as firing from the British cannons stopped
and someone answered their astonishment,
    "It means the infantry is coming up!"

Chapter 5

Bunker Hill: The Red Waves
June 17, 1775

As Colonel Prescott stood upon the berm
  he signaled down to men upon the beach
by pointing his drawn saber up the shore
  at the approaching British infantry.

The British in command was General Howe
  who planned to turn the Patriots' left flank
and smash them on the beach with one strong blow
  and watch the ragtag rebels scatter ranks.

He sent 10 companies of infantry
  in rank and file of soldiers 4 abreast
to march along the Mystic River beach
  and put the insurrection to a rest.

When the unruly rebels turned to run
  his infantry would then block the retreat
and then the day would easily be won
  when all his other forces ran a sweep.

John Stark was the commanding officer
  of Patriots positioned on the beach.
The regiment had built a stone breastwork
  and stood with loaded muskets 3 rows deep.

The ammunition that they had was scarce
  and Colonel Stark had emphasized control.
He sternly made it absolutely clear
  they follow orders to stand firm and hold.

The soldiers had to stay composed and wait
   until they looked the British in the eye
and listened out to hear the Colonel say
   the drill of arms to "Ready, aim and fire."

The Patriots all stood attentively.
   They heard the tapping tension of the drum
and saw the redcoats marching up the beach.
   Then one of the men noted, "Here they come."

No one can say it is an easy task
   to keep a flintlock steady at his side
when a whole army was approaching fast
   with the intent to take his mortal life.

And Colonel Stark was shouting to his soldiers
   to steady them, reminding them to hold,
like standing in the path of rolling boulders
   as Britain's army marched in its approach.

At 90 yards the Patriots stood firm.
   At 80 yards some twitched with nervous grins.
At 70 their heartbeats could be heard.
   At 60 Stark then called out to his men —

He called attention to the soldiers' ranks.
   He ordered the front row to lift their guns.
The hammers clicked as soldiers took their aim
   and with Stark's word the front all fired at once.

The men then followed training of the drill.
   They did not gawk until the smoke was clear.
This was no time for soldiers to stand still.
   The front row had to move back to the rear.

Clear in the back, the first set to reload
    and the next line then stepped up to the front
and sternly steadied in a well-dressed row,
    they heard the order to lift up their guns.

The regiment then kept a steady fire
    and poured the musket shot in blow by blow
and as each company came into sight
    they mowed down British soldiers row by row.

Upon the beach the wounded and the dead
    were blocking regulars from marching through.
They had been wedged into a bottle neck
    and so the British infantry withdrew.

Howe failed in his attempt to turn the flank
    by thrusting a spearhead along the shore
but infantry used in the beach attack
    was just a fraction of the British force.

Then Prescott watched the British troops below
    and Howe positioned for a full assault.
Howe planned to strike an overwhelming blow
    and press the rebels in a toppled fall.

Then three large columns of the regulars
    set off to march in an outspread array.
The line spanned the entire peninsula
    — the wave of an approaching hurricane.

At left the grenadiers were on the march
    and stamping over meadows in advance
and Prescott signaled Captain Knowlton's guard
    whose men entrenched with railing from a fence.

At right marines were coming in long files
    by Charlestown's neat rows of homes and streets
to try attacking from the town's hillside
    and turn the redoubt's strength defensively.

Then marching front and center was the mass
    of infantry that stretched across the field
with glinting bayonets and shiny brass
    to surge a wave of red to rush the hill.

They knew what they must do in the redoubt.
    The ammunition was in short supply.
They had to make sure every shot would count
    and fight with all their might to hold the line.

Then peering over the redoubt's dirt wall
    they watched the British army in their march
with tapping drums and the commanders' calls
    that steadily were sounding from afar.

But then they noticed British grenadiers,
    who marched upon the pastures at the left,
were held up by the natural barriers
    as swampy ground was bogging down their steps.

Then fences further cumbered their advance
    and obstacles disorganized their lines
and they were holding up the British plan
    and bungled up the strategy's design.

Then marksmen Prescott had sent formerly
    were set in Charlestown and taking aim
and chipped away the columns of marines
    by picking off the soldiers in their ranks.

Then groups of the marines had to detach
    to find the snipers causing the delay
and on the right the column was held back
    as the marine approach was held at bay.

Yet central columns of the infantry
    that were the main deployment of the force
were marching and advancing steadily
    as the main body kept a well-aimed course.

The outstretched ranks of British regulars
    were stamping heavy boots upon the ground
while rising up the slope in cadenced march,
    converging on the Patriot redoubt.

The Patriots were lined up at the wall
    with loaded flintlocks set upon the berm
and Doctor Warren and the Colonel called
    the men with steady, reassuring words.

The British certainly were drawing near
    but Patriots were holding the hilltop.
The orders that they had were crystal clear
    and they could not afford to take potshots.

The British regulars marched up the hill.
    The pressure was intense with the approach.
The Patriots were standing firm and still
    till they could count the buttons on the coats.

Then Prescott yelled with an authority,
    "First volley — Ready! — Steady! —Aim your sights,"
the pause then spanned for an eternity,
    then Colonel William Prescott yelled out, "Fire!"

Then as they drilled, they alternated time
    while synchronized with Prescott's strong command
and kept the rhythm of a steady fire
    while slamming volleys from their hilltop stand.

The British march was brought to a full stop
    but regulars were bravely taking aim
and the courageous British stood and fought
    while Patriots were blowing them away.

And on both sides the valiant soldiers fell
    while the alarms were beating on the drums.
The Patriots were struck by shot and shell
    and Doctor Warren tried to staunch the blood.

Then British drums began to beat retreat
    and carnage on the field was terrible.
And both the grenadiers and the marines
    joined with the infantry in the withdrawal.

The British soldiers reset on the shore
    and Prescott watched to see what they would do.
Then leaving Boston there were more transports
    and it was clear the British were not through.

The Patriots then saw the rising smoke
    that grew into a billowing dark storm
as flames began to spread through rows of homes
    and British soldier started to reform.

Some shouted out, "They're burning down the town!"
    and many asked to go and douse the flames
but regulars were coming back around
    and Prescott ordered them to stay in place.

They saw the leaping flames and clouds of smoke
    from the redoubt upon the tiny mound,
but soldiers cannot leave their ordered posts
    no matter if their homes are burning down.

The soldiers' ammunition was then low.
    The British infantry was coming up.
The dry, warm inland wind began to blow
    and the whole town was starting to combust.

The Patriots then followed the strict drill
    and carefully aimed every single shot.
Then out of shot they tried to hold the hill
    by picking up the stones and hurling rocks.

Then British regulars stood on the berm
    and Patriots tried making one last stand
and then the order of retreat was heard
    — they could not fight the British with bare hands.

As Colonel Prescott made sure they were clear
    he signaled Doctor Warren to retreat
and as they both were moving to the rear
    a bullet killed the Doctor instantly.

And redcoats rushed in like a fiery sea
    while storming over the redoubts breastwork
and Colonel Prescott covered the retreat
    parlaying bayonets with his drawn sword.

The reinforcements had arrived below
    and held the regulars from a pursuit.
The sun had set. The bloody day had closed
    and orderly the Patriots withdrew.

Throughout the night the local buildings burned,
   the churches' steeples toppled in the flames
and family homes and years of earnest work
   were lost along with soldiers' lives that day.

The Patriots had made a valiant stand
   and showed the British army they could fight,
but Boston lost a great American
   when Doctor Joseph Warren gave his life.

Chapter 6

The Continental Army
July 2 – 4, 1775

At Boston Bay the 2nd of July
   some men on horses rode into the camp
without parade, announcement or design
   to indicate appointment of command.

George Washington had wanted to observe
   the true conditions of the gathered troops
and inconspicuously he could learn
   their state before an orderly review.

What General Washington was riled to find
   were soldiers set in camps in disarray.
There was no structure of a rank and file
   with patchwork lines positioned at the bay.

New Englanders had mustered a large force,
   deployed from the surrounding colonies
but the arrangement was in dire discord
   without assigned responsibilities.

The insubordination was enflamed
   without a code of conduct for the men
and soldiers often shouted out in rage
   that showed the lack of any discipline.

The soldiers lived in a disgusting filth
   without a sense of health or good hygiene.
There was a lack of exercise and drill
   and officers were ragged and demeaned.

A soldier's work is certainly not clean
    while holding a position in a trench
but General Washington had to redeem
    the soldiers with a sense of self-respect.

But soldiers' self-respect is not through ease,
    it is the work of tireless polishing
with self-control that is unfaltering
    while pushing every day to build up strength.

And General Washington rode stoically,
    accompanied by his commanding staff
and what he felt and thought, no one could see,
    he was completely focused on his task.

At Cambridge sentries questioned Washington
    and then the General nodded to his staff
announcing the appointment of command
    by Continental Congress delegates.

Then General Washington spoke to the sentries
    requesting the top ranking officers.
He promptly needed to arrange a meeting
    with the three Generals – Putnam, Schuyler, Ward.

Then Washington was led to Harvard Yard
    at the 1st college of the colonies,
a treasure Patriots set out to guard
    for the enrichment of posterity.

Soon after ranking officers arrived
    and when the introductions had been made,
the officers reviewed defensive lines
    set like a horseshoe round the Boston Bay.

They rode to batteries on Prospect Hill
    directly to the south of Mystic River
within a cannon's range from Bunker Hill
    where British soldiers had dug fresh entrenchments.

And Washington saw Charlestown was razed,
    the fire destroyed each business, church and home,
and only chimneys had survived the blaze
    that marked the ashy graves like brick tombstones.

After the Patriots had to retreat
    from the redoubt on the peninsula,
the British forces built up batteries
    to fortify the neck of Charlestown.

And with entrenchments dug on Bunker Hill
    the redcoats mounted their artillery
to cannonade a mile of open field
    and hold back the encroachments of the siege.

Below, the officers saw the entrenchments
    where the advance position had been dug
and Patriots were shooting at the British
    far out of range of any soldier's gun.

Then Washington said to the officers
    "Those men are wasting precious ammunition.
We need to hold our powder in reserve
    and they are giving up their held position.

"Those men must know to not discharge their guns
    with the exception of direct defense.
Such carelessness is not how wars are won.
    We must have unity and discipline."

The group then travelled for at least 8 miles
    from north down to Roxbury in the south,
so Washington inspected the whole line
    and met the officers at each redoubt.

The British had the powder and the lead
    with a full armory and arsenal
but they could not keep all the soldiers fed
    confined on Boston's small peninsula.

The Patriots had built up a defense
    to try to keep the British force contained
and blocked the Charlestown and Boston necks
    from any land advance of a foray.

The British forces could control the sea
    and they could send out numbers of transports
to swarm the shore with columns of marines
    and strike the Patriots at any point.

So General Washington had the livestock
    drove far from shore deep in the countryside
beyond the reach of any raid's attack
    that could replenish British food supplies.

Then Washington set to secure the line
    with a strong sense of uniformity
and formed consistency of a design
    from motley regiments of colonies.

Then Washington gave orders to the ranks
    with clear communication through the lines
to execute the military way
    from top to bottom for each lightning strike.

And Washington set General Lee at left
    with a strong force of men in his command
to block the British set at Charlestown
    from an assault they may attempt by land.

And General Ward was in command at right
    to strengthen the Roxbury batteries
and block a march into the countryside
    so British could be held under the siege.

Then General Putnam was placed in the center
    to guard the landing on Back Bay's shore side
with the Connecticut militia soldiers
    and hold together the extending line.

Then General Washington ordered a count
    of the provisions, armaments and men,
ensuring that the enterprise was sound
    with practicality and common sense.

July 4 Washington took the command
    and issued his first set of General Orders
to clarify conduct and tasks at hand
    with the specific duties of the soldiers.

The men must set aside their rivalries
    and operate as one in unity.
They were far more than men from colonies.
    Their great and common cause was liberty.

They had assembled to defend their country
    and vowed to fight at arms courageously.
They then composed the Continental Army.
    Together they would claim the victory.

Chapter 7

Slow Work and Urgent Needs
July – December 1775

For months the Boston siege was a stalemate
   as General Washington repaired the line.
The soldiers had to be on guard and wait
   to look out for a raid at any time.

The passages upon the necks of land
   were fortified by British regiments
and sensibly of General Washington
   he ruled out an attack on battlements.

If he attempted a direct assault
   to concentrate on British batteries,
the Patriots would then be forced to charge
   into the enemy's defensive strength.

They would be torn apart by British fire
   and gunships would then rake the open field
and they would never reach the British line
   and countless soldiers would be lost and killed.

The siege was weakening the British force
   as the containment took a steady toll
but people are impatient of slow work
   with popular demands for quick results.

The Patriots were restless for some gains
   and Continental Congress would demand
a way to measure progress for each day
   with numbered figures they could understand.

The British had been eating the milk cows
   and tearing up the wharves to burn as fuel.
They were exhausting the supplies in town
   and would be forced to exercise a move.

Time was a factor Washington knew well
   and waiting is a burden tough to bear.
The soldiers would be sore to keep details
   with their enlistments ending with the year.

Most of the soldiers signed on for 6 months
   and stepped up for America's defense
but if they left when their short term was done
   there would not be an army without them.

Then Washington and Congress would be forced
   to raise another army once again
and they would be beleaguered in the war
   with raw recruits that needed to be trained.

The seasoned soldiers are rare elements
   with mettle tempered with experience
that drill has honed and sharpened with an edge
   and finished with a polished discipline.

The veterans know how to work together,
   coordinating through their unity
in the subordination to commanders
   combining all their strength effectively.

Not every soldier has the same assignment
   but soldiers have to know and own their jobs
and all the different pieces work together
   to move with the precision of a clock.

There were small ships that had been armed with cannons
    the Patriots deployed as privateers,
and hunted ships that might supply provisions
    although they could not fend off man-o'-wars.

One ship had captured a supply transport
    with loads of shot along with a brass mortar
and held at least 2000 new flintlocks
    although it didn't carry any powder.

And this small victory improved morale
    to lift and boost the Patriots' esteem
and the new British muskets were passed out
    that many soldiers needed desperately.

Then Washington considered Bunker Hill
    that Patriots fought for courageously
and although they were driven from the field
    the British had a Pyrrhic victory.

The British army lost 1000 men
    — at least one half of what they had deployed,
and this depleted their whole garrison
    and neutralized a quarter of their force.

What more, the Patriots had nearly won,
    the soldiers had been holding the redoubt
and if the reinforcements had come up
    the loads of shot would not have given out.

The reinforcements had been raw recruits
    who skittishly would not charge up the hill
but if they had joined up with Prescott's troops
    the combination would have won the field.

The reinforcements covered the retreat
    and held the British soldiers at the neck
but they were at the door of victory
    if the reserves had properly been led.

If General Howe had lost his 3rd assault
    it is unlikely he'd have launched a 4th.
Howe would have had no choice but to withdraw
    and transport in defeat to Boston's wharves.

Then if the Patriots had held the ground
    at Charlestown on the peninsula,
the set artillery in the redoubt
    would have secured advantage from above.

With Boston rendered indefensible
    the British could not hold up in the bay.
Their post would then have been untenable.
    They would have been forced to evacuate.

Of course those matters made no difference then.
    The chance was gone. The battle had been lost.
The changing situations never end
    yet some scenarios are similar.

By setting up a post in the redoubt
    they had performed a key strategic ploy,
compelling British forces to come out
    into the open where they're vulnerable.

George Washington looked south to Dorchester.
    The hills were overlooking Boston neck.
The British hold would be untenable
    if they could mount their cannons on the crest.

But all the cannons at their batteries
   were needed to support the siege's line.
They could not render any point too weak
   where the containment could be compromised.

Then Washington considered Lake Champlain
   where the old Fort Ticonderoga set.
If they could bring those cannons to the bay
   they'd gain the upper hand for an offense.

The problem was the rugged, wild terrain.
   The fort was in the mountains to the north
and icy weather was not far away.
   The brutal job would battle winter storms.

Then General Washington met with his staff
   and they decided Colonel Henry Knox
would lead a group for this important task
   and in November the campaign set off.

Although the Colonel had been a bookseller
   he had become a soldier for the cause
and proved to be ingenious in endeavors
   for the artillery's important jobs.

He handled the logistics with deft ease,
   could read terrain for the strategic plots
and knots of Gordian he skillfully
   would solve with a quick flash of cannon shot.

Then as the campaign was well underway
   George Washington attended to the troops.
The fabric of the army could not fray.
   When times were bad, he had to lead them through.

1776

Chapter 8

The Narrow Path of Freedom
January 1776

On January 1 George Washington
    had issued a new set of General Orders
ensuring everyone would understand
    the expectations of the Army's soldiers.

Maintaining a sharp state of vigilance
    requires the constant work of preparation
and the direction of due diligence
    necessitates precise communications.

There is no room for ambiguity
    in the conduct of martial operations
and the bewildering contingencies
    harass with never ending complications.

The ships that sail upon the peaceful seas
    can wave their flags in the refreshing breeze
appearing in a state of leisure ease
    and set their course wherever as they please.

But sailing ships cannot control the seas
    and there is never any guarantee
that storms will not erupt chaotically
    and crews must manage their own buoyancy.

A soldier always readies for a storm,
    no matter if the skies are clear and calm.
It is too late to brace against the harm
    when lightning strikes and winds rush in a squall.

There are horizons of the unforeseen
    with rife complexities beyond foresight.
For the assurance that a ship won't sink
    the shielding hull must stay both strong and tight.

With the new year George Washington confirmed
    the conduct for the course they were embarking
and all the soldiers proudly were assured
    that they composed the Continental Army.

The torch may have been lit in Lexington
    but this was more than a New England cause.
They fought for freedom of America
    and all the colonies were then involved.

New Englanders had bravely shown their strength
    by mustering militias in the towns
and farther south the crack shot riflemen
    had marched to Boston with George Washington.

In Philadelphia where Congress met
    the representing statesmen made decrees
and every colony sent delegates
    confirming strength in formal unity.

King George III had made a formal speech
    and vowed to crush the colonies' rebellion.
He'd force the colonies down to their knees
    as helpless subjects of the King of England.

From Maine to Georgia in America
    the people were determined to be free
and faith and virtue can rise up above
    with willingness to work for liberty.

Yet freedom's not whatever people want.
    It does not guarantee what people need.
It only is obtained at a great cost
    and cannot be sustained haphazardly.

And although liberty may open ways
    for people to pursue their lofty dreams,
their freedom is a path to gain their aims
    but they must focus their abilities.

And focus isn't an all seeing vision
    of a miraculous, anointed gift.
It is determination of intention
    applied through rigorous self-discipline.

And in the statement Washington was clear
    — they must have regularity and order.
They shouldered what most others dare not bear.
    The men were not civilians. They were soldiers.

The soldier kept up exercise and drill
    and Washington worked to retain his men
while keeping quiet his plan for the hill
    at Dorchester above the battlements.

There was concern the British would advance
    before the cannons could arrive with Knox.
The Patriots could lose another chance
    to gain a key to open the deadlock.

The winter freeze was gnashing icy teeth.
    The snow upon the mountains would be deep.
The haul of shot and cannons was a feat
    that might not be delivered until spring.

The General could not wait for one long shot.
    There are no certainties in life and war.
There is no script with an exclusive plot.
    Great plans have tendencies to fall apart.

So Washington took count of what he had
    and carefully considered what to do.
They had to seize what was within their grasp
    while keeping new developments in view.

He feinted some attacks across the ice,
    built force near Bunker Hill to make a bluff
and turned attention from Dorchester Heights
    so Howe would concentrate at Charlestown.

His watches spotted infantry embark
    on British ships that sailed from Boston Bay
suggesting Howe might try to seize New York
    and in the spring time launch a new campaign.

If General Howe controlled the Hudson Bay
    the British fleet would then command the river
and Washington sent General Lee that way
    to guard New York with a strong force of soldiers.

Then late in January Colonel Knox
    fulfilled a truly Herculean feat
by hauling tons of cannons with the shot
    across the snow on sleds with oxen teams.

George Washington could not have been more pleased
    to move upon the British garrison.
They had possession of the crucial piece.
    They were prepared to execute the plan.

Chapter 9

Dorchester Heights
January – March 1776

The winter tried the Continental Army
 when soldiers' terms of service were complete.
The losses of their numbers were alarming
 and they were straining to sustain their strength.

From Bunker Hill the British batteries
 were often firing heavy shot and bombs
but without stockpiles of the armories
 the hunkered Patriots could not respond.

When the rebellion battles had begun
 the men enlisted to join in the fight
then scarcity of powder for their guns
 required the men to strictly hold their fire.

So as the British lobbed annoying rounds,
 abusing Patriots both day and night,
resolve for many began wearing down
 — by holding fire, the men burned up inside.

The tents in camps were filled with choking smoke
 where wearied soldiers could not breath or sleep
then outside in the wind and bitter cold
 their tattered coats exposed them to the freeze.

Some clapboard barracks were built for the men
 to try to ease the brutal misery
but while on guard in trenches frozen stiff
 the men took British insults silently.

And as enlistment terms came to an end
    some of the soldiers were returning home.
They had their farms and families to tend
    so seeds of the next season could be sown.

So in the face of a strong enemy
    the Army was refitted and reformed
and this had to be done clandestinely
    so weak points in the line would not be stormed.

The 8 miles Patriots had to defend
    were often dangerously undermanned.
If Howe had known how weak some posts had been
    the British could have marched straight in their camps.

But many of the soldiers had stepped up,
    resolved to see the whole endeavor through.
They could not leave important tasks undone
    and so the Army's numbers were renewed.

Although George Washington could not announce
    the major operation that was near,
the soldiers chose to hold defenses down
    with nothing but the prospects of despair.

And even without any sign of hope
    to make the ordeal easier to bear,
the men continued to endure the cold
    and re-enlisted for another year.

The key then was to time the strategy
    for the best opportunity to strike.
George Washington could not wait till the spring.
    They must move forward or they'd fall behind.

The British certainly would not stand still.
  In springtime operations would resume.
Their stores and garrison would be refilled
  and General Howe could stage to make a move.

The English ships were blocked by winter storms
  from crossing the Atlantic Ocean's span.
By spring they could build up a stronger force
  and march their columns for assaults on land.

The Patriots must strike the British first
  before the opportunity had closed
but Washington could not declare a word
  until the operation was deployed.

So Washington assigned specific tasks
  while feinting northward near the Mystic River
and sent small raids intended to harass
  with misdirection from his planned endeavor.

Inland beyond Roxbury to the south
  the soldiers were discretely felling trees
and gathered up the scattered logs and rocks
  for what was certainly a mystery.

For months the men were ordered to reserve
  the small supply of powder that they had
and what the Army managed to conserve
  could then be used for a decisive blast.

George Washington made sure not to repeat
  the fatal error that they made before.
The soldiers would have all the shot they'd need
  to hold position from the British force.

When batteries were set at Dorchester
   the British redcoats would have to respond
and when the British tried to storm the fort
   his men would be prepared for them to come.

George Washington still kept his plan concealed
   and had the men discretely store supplies.
They all had thought he aimed for Bunker Hill
   while Washington disguised the grand design.

The ground was frozen over two feet deep.
   The ice remained on portions of the bay.
The Patriots had all that they would need
   and Washington set matters underway.

The leading officers were then informed
   of the assignments for each company
and Colonel Knox was ordered to report
   and was assigned to build the battery.

Since ground was frozen solid on the hill,
   they'd have to shield the guns with gabions
and all the timber that the soldiers felled
   would frame large baskets holding rocks and logs.

The 2nd day of March they lit the fuse
   with a diversionary cannonade
by feinting Bunker Hill to make a ruse
   so General Howe would turn his strength that way.

The cannon fire continued for 3 days
   and after sunset on the 4th of March
far to the right across the Boston Bay
   the operation was off to its start.

Each man had been assigned specific jobs
    and they all knew exactly what to do.
The plans and orders had been clearly drawn
    and everyone was synchronized in queue.

The sky was flashing with a martial storm
    as cannon thunder rolled across the bay
and Colonel Knox led a strong army corps
    to haul the guns and shot on wooden sleighs.

They hauled those cannons through the mountain snow
    up icy slopes to crest each alpine pass
then tumbled into valleys down below
    and dug out from the snow banks that collapsed.

The hills of Dorchester could not compare
    with the steep mountains in the countryside
yet still the job was not an easy fare
    — they had to have the cannons set that night.

So in the dark they labored urgently
    as loads of heavy metal was conveyed
with officers directing in the lead
    as the artillery was set in place.

The timbers, rocks and logs were close behind
    and gabions were built around the guns.
Together they completed the design
    before the twilight of the morning sun.

And Colonel Knox along with all his men
    admired the most magnificent sunrise
while looking down on British battlements
    with loaded cannons in the early light.

The water on the Boston Bay was calm.
    The sky was blue with clouds of rosy pink
and Colonel Knox sent out the morning call
    to stir the British soldiers from their sleep.

Then all the cannons joined in jubilee.
    The Patriots were taking back their town
as British soldiers scrambled frantically
    while bombs and iron shot came raining down.

The British began loading their transports
    to move to Dorchester for an assault
but in the afternoon a sudden storm
    forced them to call the operation off.

Yet even in the storm on the hilltop
    the Patriots kept building up their strength
continuing to haul munitions up,
    they would not be removed from the hill's seat.

They had retained command at Boston Bay.
    They would not suffer under tyrants' tread
and for 6 days they kept the cannonade
    while dropping bombs upon the redcoats' heads.

Chapter 10

Changing Posts
March – April 1776

The Patriots allowed the smoke to clear
    and Howe sent messages to Washington
with the intention to withdraw declared
    for the evacuation of the town.

And Howe made an appeal for soldier's honor
    and said the town would not be set ablaze
if British soldiers were not bombed while loading
    so British ships could safely get away.

The Patriots had aimed to free the town
    but did not want the British to escape
yet would they let their precious town burn down
    or let the British fight another day?

George Washington decided to relent,
    for the assurance Boston was not razed
then Patriots could build a strong defense
    ensuring Boston stayed secure and safe.

Then Washington sent orders to his men
    as consequences of war are profound,
he would not suffer lack of discipline
    — just one loose cannon could destroy the town.

Some men were puzzled why they must resist
    the passion that insisted on no quarters,
but Washington demanded excellence
    — a soldier's job is to obey his orders.

The 17th of March the British force
   went rushing through the town chaotically
and crowded on the ships docked at the wharves
   and hastily withdrew in a retreat.

A thousand men who had survived small pox
   marched into Boston at the column's head
after the boats departed from the docks
   as Boston was infected with the plague.

The British army had withdrawn in haste
   and barracks and defenses were deserted
and stores and cannons had been cast away
   that could be salvaged and brought back in service.

The Patriots employed to fortify.
   There was no time for them to celebrate.
They could not let the opening slip by
   to strengthen the defenses of the bay.

Then the inspection of the town had proved
   that houses and possessions were secured.
There was some damage from billeted troops
   but Boston fortunately was preserved.

Then Washington wrote John Hancock a letter
   to let the President of Congress know
that Boston had been freed from British fetters
   and they were guarding the New England homes.

The British ships were anchored near the harbor
   to fit for sea before they left the bay
and he would keep the body of the Army
   in Boston till the British sailed away.

They'd fortify the hilltops guarding Boston
    to be maintained by the militia troops.
The Army would then march into position
    anticipating General Howe's next move.

George Washington knew where Howe would move next.
    The British would sail to the Hudson Bay.
They'd try to cut the colonies in half
    with gunships on the Hudson River way.

The British wanted to block off New England
    from contact with the other colonies,
then broke in half the movement would be weakened
    and keep the people subjects of the King.

The Patriots lacked ships to build a navy
    to nautically contend with British might.
They'd have to block the passage with the Army
    with batteries along the riverside.

The Hudson River gave communication
    to British forces inside Canada
and would allow the threats from two directions
    to move with ease in the interior.

And New York City was a prize and treasure
    — the biggest city in the colonies,
with wharves and docks and an expansive harbor
    where British could maintain their naval fleet.

Then on the 27th day of March
    the British ships sailed to the open sea
and General Washington ordered a march
    to move supplies and soldiers orderly.

Each day he would dispatch a whole brigade
    and space each group to keep a steady pace
then rode ahead along the Army's flank
    to check terrain while scouting to survey.

Then as the line of infantry arrived
    he designated each strategic place
and ordered the assignments of the files
    to carefully unpack the soldiered ranks.

The Army had at least 10,000 men
    with wagon loads of gear and food in tow.
They needed places to set up their tents
    and needed orders to know where to go.

When General Lee had been sent months before
    he set a battery on Brooklyn Heights
for the defense of the deep water port
    before the British gunships would arrive.

Then as he organized the Army's men
    a message from the Continental Congress
required a meeting with George Washington
    in Philadelphia with urgent promptness.

Chapter 11

To Form a New Government
May 1776

In Philadelphia Congress was pleased
    and General Washington was cheered with praise
accepting the ovation stoically
    — the Continental Army won the day.

Yet other matters urgently impressed
    with dire uncertainty of coming days
and countless details had to be addressed
    for the asserted cause to be sustained.

For decades the discussions of complaints
    and printed pamphlets with the arguments
provided the perspectives of debate
    for the petitions of their grievances.

They were not begging for some charity,
    the colonists had prospered for sometime
but Crown and Parliament made policies
    that violated people's natural rights.

The colonists had long been self-sustained,
    developed towns and local governments.
They cultivated farms that were maintained
    and were protected by their own defense.

But without recognition of their rights
    and their appeals censured by Parliament,
they had become embroiled in a dire fight
    from the attacks of British government.

The question was how to protect their rights
    for their pursuits in life through liberty
and some thought matters could be reconciled
    yet most insisted on self-sovereignty.

If Patriots decided to relent
    to sovereignty of Crown and Parliament,
they'd lie down to a foreign government
    and only gain what George III would give.

Suppressive acts denied the colonies
    protection from the ruling English Crown
so then both logically and legally
    the colonies were rendered on their own.

The acts of Parliament had made decrees
    denying them the rights of Englishmen
and independence of the colonies
    must be sustained with their own government.

John Adams had drawn a concise outline
    for the establishment of a Republic
devoted to protecting natural rights
    and dedicated to the common people.

The powers were drawn in discrete divisions
    — executive, judicial, legislative —
with delegates appointed by decisions
    determined through the popular elections.

The colonies were writing constitutions
    based on the outline Adams had proposed
and Congress planned for a Confederation
    so an established unity would hold.

Yet still the men were not in full agreement
    and some held hope for reconciliation
and they resisted making the commitment
    required to build an independent nation.

And some hoped France or Spain would recognize
    the independence of the colonies
and then they would have others on their side
    for the support of their self-sovereignty.

And other then vehemently replied
    how that obtuse position was absurd,
they cannot wait for others to decide —
    the people must decide for themselves first.

The soldiers of the Continental Army
    weren't fighting to be subjects of the King.
The people of the colonies were arming
    and boldly fighting so they could be free.

They had refused to bow to tyranny
    and their self-government was their intention,
then for the bell of liberty to ring
    the Congress must declare their independence.

Then Washington provided a report
    for what they did and what still must be done,
gave an assessment of the Army's force
    and then he promptly rode back to the front.

Chapter 12

Strategies and Contingencies
June 1776

When General Washington returned to camp
    he noted how the ranks of men had grown
with new enlistments joining in the stand
    defending their own country and their homes.

The new recruits were lined up on Broadway
    and exercised the manual of arms
as sergeants watched the lines of the closed ranks
    correcting the infractions as they marched.

Most of the men already were crack shots
    — could nail a squirrel on the tips of trees,
but there is more a person must be taught
    to work as soldiers in tight unity.

The new recruits were moving awkwardly
    through how the Army strictly operates
and drilling manuals repeatedly
    they learned to live the military way.

The soldiers and the flintlocks would combine
    as soldiers and their arms were more than friends.
The flintlocks were part of the soldiers' lives,
    familiar as their torso and their limbs.

And in each unit they would synchronize
    as crucial parts that made a larger body
to live and eat and work and drill and fight
    together as the Continental Army.

Then on his steed the General would approach
    and officers would stop and snap salutes
and excellence was the determined goal
    as General Washington reviewed the troops.

The men were also building batteries
    and pushing heavy cannons into place
to set the Patriots' artillery
    defending New York and the Hudson Bay.

Yet there was great concern for the position.
    The Army was divided on the islands
and with the large fleet of the British frigates
    the Patriots would have a disadvantage.

The movements of an army are a challenge
    with obstacles and problems to attend
especially when officers must fathom
    traversing waterways without a bridge.

They held positions on strategic points
    anticipating routes of the advance
but then the British could use their transports
    to launch attacks on miles of river banks.

The Brooklyn Heights were strongly fortified
    providing the port's principal defenses
and overlooked the New York harbor side
    with guns positioned over the East River.

And at the north point of Manhattan Island
    they watched up river from Fort Washington
and added to the strength of the position
    with a division at the garrison.

Then in New York there were three more divisions
    that were prepared to move at an alarm
and post at any shore along the island
    where British troops may try to disembark.

The number of the troops had almost doubled.
    The Army stood with 20,000 men
with the enlistment of courageous people
    who took up arms for liberty's defense.

The General reckoned the contingencies
    while waiting for the British to arrive.
The Army was positioned dangerously
    but could not leave New York without a fight.

While meeting with the Continental Congress
    there was one point where everyone agreed
— without the Army they would be defenseless
    and would be forced to yield to tyranny.

The Congressmen and soldiers staked their lives
    for commonwealth for all posterity
and each one of them was prepared to die
    for principles upholding liberty.

This was not just a malcontent rebellion.
    They aimed to build a model government
to stand up for the rights of all the people
    for life and the pursuit of happiness.

George Washington was wielding a bright sword.
    He had command of national defense
and with the Continental Army's corps
    the people and the cause relied on him.

In Congress they will bicker endlessly
    debating different points of policy
but armies operate like a machine
    with grit and grind and tireless polishing.

And Washington was burdened with the weight
    but did not speak of what set on his shoulders.
Whatever rank, the duty is the same
    — a soldier's job is to obey his orders.

Then tragic news from northern troops arrived,
    the Patriots withdrew from Canada
and British threatened from another side
    and Washington might have to fight two fronts.

And Congress was not able to agree
    to make a vote declaring independence.
Were they free states or simply colonies?
    Were they at war or just in a rebellion?

The 29th of June a ship arrived,
    most certainly the flagship of the fleet,
with British colors flying up on high
    and set the anchors far from cannon's reach.

A cannon then resounded with a boom
    and many people saw the cloud of smoke
as the flagship discharged a loud salute
    with the appearance of another boat.

Then once again they heard a loud report
    come rolling over waters on the bay
as yet another boat came into port
    with British colors waving in display.

Again, again they heard the gun's salutes
　　and people gathered in the streets in awe
and many climbed to perch on houses' roofs
　　and were incredulous of what they saw.

For hours the ships of war were tacking sails
　　into the bay and anchored with the fleet
and by the afternoon no one could tell
　　the number of the ships set distantly.

And many stood astonished and bewildered
　　at the flotilla that arrived that day
then Washington said women and the children
　　must be made ready to evacuate.

Chapter 13

Declaring Independence
July 1776

The noncombatants readied to leave town
   and shelter in the tranquil countryside.
The Army had dug in to hold the ground
   and they were bound for a colossal fight.

Upon the docks and from surrounding hills
   the Patriots kept watch of British moves
so when the British set upon the field
   they'd gain a general number of the troops.

The ships were anchored 8 miles from the town
   in clear view of the people of New York
and although soldiers had not touched the ground
   they obviously brought an awesome force.

They all knew of the Boston victory
   and how the British were pressed to retreat.
This time the British brought a naval fleet
   with countless tons of their artillery.

And next to Staten Island on the bay
   at least a hundred warships had been set
and in the brilliant light of summer days
   the masts looked like a million bayonets.

The 2nd of July they disembarked
   at least 10,000 of the British ranks
and more transports and gunships were not far
   and 20,000 more were on the way.

And Washington sent orders to his men
    preparing for an imminent attack.
They had prepared the strength of their defense
    to hold advances of the British back.

And General Washington was well aware
    the only chance they had for victory
was if the Army's soldiers were prepared
    and stood with order and in unity.

The 9th a happy courier appeared
    — the vote in Congress was unanimous!
The country's independence was declared
    and on the 4th they signed the document.

Then Washington unrolled the parchment sheet
    and thoughtfully took time to closely read
— the script proclaimed the country's liberty
— the People of America were free.

A government is for the populace
    so people may pursue their happiness.
The people are not for a government
    to plunder people's own development.

And then the document gave a clear list
    of the abuses made by British rule.
The People were why government exists.
    They were not government's subjects and tools.

America's united colonies
    developed their own government and trade
and capable of self-sufficiency
    they were made free and independent states.

In time the 56 state delegates
  of Continental Congress had all signed
for freedom of the People which they staked
  their sacred honor, fortunes and their lives.

They were defending their own liberty.
  They were in the control of their own fate.
They were no longer the King's colonies.
  They were a nation of United States.

Then General Washington called up his staff
  to make transcriptions of the document
so that the news may be dispersed and passed
  to every soldier in the regiments.

George Washington made sure the hardy troops
  who had enlisted in the Army's corps
without a doubt completely understood
  exactly what they all were fighting for.

The officers then read before the men
  as soldiers solemnly stood at attention
and heard the statements of the document
  — the Declaration of their Independence.

But independence is not something read.
  It is not something that is wrote or signed.
There was no matter in what had been said
  what British gunships would not recognize.

The People's independence is declared
  in how the People's freedom is sustained
and the unscrupulous without a care
  will let their freedom swiftly slip away.

That night New York began to celebrate
  and people were swept off in revelry
and living in a liberated state
  they exercised their freedom as they pleased.

They plundered Tory houses recklessly
  and piled debris for bonfires in the streets
then feeling justified with spiteful glee
  the riot mobbed about at Bowling Green.

Then crowding round the cast of George III
  they fell the statue of the British King
and swarmed the city like unruly herds
  intoxicated with wild anarchy.

George Washington gave orders for his men
  to strictly keep their quarters in their camps.
They could not drop the guard of their defense
  less they would be severely disciplined.

The riot was a dismal disappointment
  in the prospects to form their government.
There would be little hope for a republic
  without the People's own self-management.

They needed more than power for success.
  They needed more than wisdom to be free.
Great power can be lost with carelessness
  and wisdom can be tempted and deceived.

For people to share common liberty
  and not inflict and suffer bleak abuse
there is an absolute necessity
  — the People must retain their Virtue too.

Then July 12 at noon two ships approached
   and rode the tide while sailing a stiff wind.
The British ships – the *Phoenix* and the *Rose*
   had cannons in the porthole openings.

The batteries began to fire out shot
   when the two British ships came into range
and both the British ships fired in response
   while passing by the batteries upstream.

And suddenly the people realized
   the British ships could launch a cannonade
and all they had including their own lives
   could be bombarded and then swept away.

The iron shot came flying into town
   and punched round holes straight through the wooden walls
and wrecked a number of the people's homes
   as they were smashed inside by cannonballs.

And people ran and shouted through the streets
   bewailing their heartbreak and wretched grief
and raved in the commotion tirelessly
   after the ships had passed the batteries.

Chapter 14

The Fire Boats
June – August 1776

The British ships had passed the batteries
   and sailed on without damage or delay
and proved the Army's vulnerability
   surrounded by deep water passageways.

The ships maneuvered to block the supplies
   that could be sent downstream from Albany
and threatened Kingsbridge from Manhattan isle
   that was the Army's one line of retreat.

George Washington had carefully secured
   3 months of rations for the Army troops
with flour and pork to last the summer tour
   and give the men a good supply of food.

And stockpiled farther up the Hudson Valley
   he had supplies of 4 months of provisions
with victuals to support the Northern Army
   in their defensive mountain pass positions.

Fort Washington along with a division
   were in position to support Kingsbridge
but with the gunships moving on the water
   the bridge would be a challenge to defend.

The Army corps was split by the East River,
   positioned at New York and Brooklyn Heights,
if they were forced to mainland to maneuver
   that bridge provided the exclusive line.

They'd heard in June a Carolina force
    repulsed a British fleet from Charleston Bay,
George Washington would try to hold New York
    to guard the vital Hudson River way.

Uncertain where the British would attack
    the General recognized two crucial threats,
they had to make sure Kingsbridge stayed intact
    and Brooklyn batteries were not upset.

George Washington positioned General Greene
    with a division of the infantry
to set 5000 men defensively
    and guard the Brooklyn Heights artillery.

But if the ships ascended the East River
    one third of all their troops would be cut off.
If there communication line was severed
    the crossing of the river would be blocked.

Then derelict sea vessels in the quays
    were tugged with pulling oars in the rowboats
and when they reached East River's channel way
    they sunk the ships so the access was closed.

Then Washington arranged another mission
    for two fire boats to move at night upstream
and find the British gunboats and their tenders
    and set for an attack clandestinely.

One of the British ships had 40 cannons,
    the other had the number of a score
and sailing with them were three schooner tenders
    with guns that added several dozen more.

The Patriots did not have any boats
    that could engage directly with the British.
With the artillery inside the holds,
    the British ships would shoot them all to pieces.

So the two boats were loaded with hay bails
    then softly paddled on a moonless night
and grappled to the ships along their rails
    and then ignited into blazing fires.

The Patriots then quickly jumped off board
    after the kindled fires were sparked and set
and quickly swam from where the ships were moored
    and hoped the fires pressed on the ships would catch.

Then pistol shots were firing from the ships
    and leaden balls were plunking in the water
as the brave men were carried with the drift
    away from the firelight into the darkness.

While treading water in the river current
    they watched the sailors frenzied work on board
and while the tiny boats were slowly burning
    the sailors tried to cut the grapple cords.

And with the raging bonfires distant light
    they saw one of the fireboats cut away
and as it sadly drifted in the night
    they saw another tender burst in flames.

The second fire boat had been a success,
    and flames began to climb the tender's ropes
then caught the mast and spread upon the deck
    and then exploded with the powder holds.

Then flying flames were arcing through the air
    after the wave of shock had bellowed out
and then the Patriots let out a cheer
    while the ship's flames were doused as it went down.

On August 18 Washington was pleased
    to see the gunships sailing hastily.
They passed the greetings of the batteries
    and quickly moved back to rejoin their fleet.

One tender that they had was not in sight
    so General Washington was confident
the fireboat mission from the former night
    must have been executed with success.

Then August 19 more ships had arrived.
    300 British ships were then in view.
The British were preparing for a strike
    and they had over 30,000 troops.

Chapter 15

The Terrible Weight
August 20–26, 1776

A few days passed without a British move
    and Patriots were strengthening their lines
by laboring in pick and shovel crews
    extending breastwork battlements for miles.

The land the Patriots had to defend
    was spread out on two islands' long expanse.
They faced a force that nearly doubled them
    with countless ways the British could advance.

They had to dig their trenches everywhere
    so they could set in various positions
since British ships could sail around the shores
    and launch attacks from numerous directions.

And the outnumbered force of Patriots
    were thinned as they were spread out on the lines
and while they worked they looked up at the boats
    for inspiration to stay energized.

They knew the boats were filled with infantry
    and grenadiers all over six feet tall
with mercenaries hired from Germany
    preparing to debouch a fierce assault.

George Washington expected the first wave
    of British disembarking on Long Island
with open space to organize their ranks
    to launch a massive ground assault offensive.

The key position was on Brooklyn Heights
    that overlooked the bay and New York harbor
but they had to support the cannon line
    cut off from the main body of the Army.

So Generals Greene and Sullivan had set
    entrenchment lines on a Long Island ridge
far out from Brooklyn Heights' East River ledge
    to meet the British forces in the field.

But with the numbers of the British soldiers
    they could sail up the Hudson River banks
and make a second landing from the water
    for an assault upon the Army's flank.

The General knew he could not set their strength
    expecting only one line of attack.
If redcoats sailed up river with their boats
    the Continental Army would be trapped.

So Washington remained beside New York
    with the main body of the Continentals,
prepared to move the central Army corps
    to counter the developing offensives.

On August 22 the transports
    set 15,000 British troops on land
at Gravesend Bay on the Long Island shore
    with General William Howe in the command.

The night before there was a raging storm
    with thunder, lightning, gale force winds and rain
and Brits and Patriots expected more
    ferocious weather on the battle range.

The air was freshened with the heavy rain,
   the farms were wafting wet and musty sod
and birds were singing in the verdant glades
   — is war defiance or an act of God?

Before the noon alarm guns sounded off
   from posts upon Red Hook and Cobble Hill
and soldiers hopped to pick up their flintlocks
   and set in their entrenchments on the field.

Each soldier looked out on the open field
   at blind bends of the roads and lines of trees
and individually each soldier felt
   the weight of terrible uncertainty.

In a long lull of the warm afternoon
   3 Patriot battalions were advanced
to reconnoiter toward the landing troops
   and get a feel for what the British planned.

And General Sullivan and General Greene
   rode out to gather the intelligence
of the front line of British infantry
   to estimate the numbers in their camps.

At 4 PM two more brigades were sent
   over the river to the Brooklyn Heights
to reinforce the batteries defense
   as a large force of British had arrived.

The 3 battalions in advance set pickets
   at Bedford, Flatbush and Gowanus Roads
and watched for any movement of the British
   to send alarm when Howe marched to approach.

At 8 PM both Sullivan and Greene
    returned and said the British were at Flatbush
and 4 miles off their line of infantry
    was digging in with fortified entrenchments.

Then Greene gave orders for the whole division
    to man their posts and keep a wary guard.
The soldiers needed to stay battle ready
    and through the night to sleep upon their arms.

The next few days were filled with skirmishes
    that drove the picket lines with brief forays
and often the sharpshooting riflemen
    would press their luck to draw some cannon play.

Off duty soldiers gathered in the shade
    to swap the stories of what they had seen
in the adventures of rambunctious raids
    while passing round some rum in a canteen.

And some would safely nap behind the hills
    that shielded them from flying musket balls
and others kept position on the field
    and waited for a chance to take a shot.

There were some fights with Hessian mercenaries
    close to Gowanus near the waterside
but there was little more than thrusts and parries
    that sputtered back and forth loose musket fire.

The British were dug in and did not move.
    The Patriots had an abundant store.
It was almost as if they made a truce.
    It seemed to be a sport more than a war.

And General Stirling set up on the right
    close to the water on Gowanus Road
and his brigade was fortifying lines
    while watching movements of the British boats.

Then General Sullivan was in command
    of the brigades at center and the left
to lead the forward line of the defense
    from Flatbush and from Bedford cross the ridge.

Reconnaissance had seen the British build
    their forces at both Bedford and Flatbush
and overtop the ridge of wooded hills
    seemed to be where they planned to make their push.

Then General Greene fell seriously ill
    and General Putnam was put in command
of the division on Long Island's field
    with British forces forming to advance.

The 26th of August Putnam moved
    more strength to both the center and the left.
The British force was building in clear view
    with the reports from the reconnaissance.

As the late afternoon turned into night
    another day came to a settled end
and pickets saw the flicker of the lights
    of countless fires that marked the British camp.

Chapter 16

The Battle of Long Island
August 27, 1776

At 6 AM on August 27
  as twilight glowed with early hints of day
upon the line's far right around Gowanus
  a roar erupted in a cannonade.

There was no need for watches to announce.
  No signal gun was needed for alarm.
The Patriots were hopping with the sounds
  of screeching shot and the exploding bombs.

And leaping from their tents set back at camp
  the men were running forward to the line
and carried flintlocks with their cartridge bags
  directly in the morning's raging fire.

The sergeants ordered soldiers to their posts
  while standing up uncovered as they yelled
and prodded stragglers who were moving slow
  more furiously than the shot and shell.

And although Stirling's men bore the attack
  the whole division stood up with their arms
and Washington could hear the booms and blasts
  and made a General Order for alarm.

Then Washington looked with his telescope
  and saw the man-o'-wars unfurling sails
and ordered guns of batteries to load,
  preparing for the port to be assailed.

And on Long Island Putnam watched the line
    with heavy firing on Gowanus Road
and had a sense that something was not right
    as most the British forces seemed to hold.

Stirling's brigade was facing Hessian men.
    Howe would not lead with German mercenaries.
The British men would spearhead an offense.
    There seemed to be some error or miscarry.

Putnam's command at both the left and center
    was standing in a still and eerie quiet.
There were no signs of any redcoat soldiers.
    The front line of the British seemed divided.

So several companies of skirmishers
    were sent to feel out for the British line
and signal when positions were confirmed
    — commanders must keep enemies in sight.

And General Stirling organized his men
    in the barrage of British cannon fire
to form the order for a strong defense
    as Hessians set to march into the fight.

Stirling's brigade had dug a strong position
    and they were braced to face a front assault
with miles of breastworks and the abatises
    along with flintlocks, powder horns and shot.

Then Stirling was surprised when Hessians stopped
    and held position beyond musket range.
They formed in columns for a forward march
    then suddenly they seemed to hesitate.

The heavy British cannonade had paused
    from batteries set far back on the field
as if allowing for a Hessian charge
    yet Hessian battle lines were standing still.

Then General Stirling told his men to wait
    till Hessian ranks moved forward to attack
and hold their fire till Hessians were in range
    and Stirling started to suspect a trap.

The warships made approaches at New York
    and Washington observed them make displays
but they were not escorting the transports
    so he suspected they were making feints.

The distant cannonade came to a halt
    and Washington supposed it was a ruse
and as the members of his staff were called
    he issued orders to prepare to move.

Then Putnam closely listened for a sign
    of sputtered fire of forward skirmishing
with the reports of muskets when they find
    the placement of the British infantry.

The cannonade was silenced to the right.
    The field was haunted with a quietness.
And then to General Putnam's dread surprise
    he heard the cannon shots sound to his left.

The shocking charge of British infantry
    was rushing at the flank and from behind
and the brigade at left was panicking
    as British bayonets ripped through the lines.

Some Patriots were trying to take aim
    but the redcoats were running through the troops.
There was a risk of hitting their own men
    as the melee grew ever more confused.

The British lined up their artillery
    and shelled the center Patriot brigade
and at Gowanus British batteries
    resumed their early morning cannonade.

The night before the British lit their fires
    for the appearance that they held their camp
then carefully withdrew to march all night
    for a surprise to hit the Army flank.

They marched for miles to reach Jamaica Pass
    then following the road across the ridge
the British marched back west for an attack
    where Patriots had not built a defense.

Then General Howe was leading a strong drive
    with charging columns of 10,000 men
directly in the Patriot's blind side
    whose left and center lines were shattering.

Then Washington knew something was amiss
    in the eruption of the roaring noise
with cannon fire and lines of musketry
    a treble sound of what it was before.

It was then clear Long Island was the front
    the British targeted for their assault.
The thundering report of heavy guns
    made clear the action on the field was hot.

George Washington gave orders to the men
   to be prepared to move without delay
if urgent reinforcements must be sent
   to cross the river at the ferry way.

Then Washington and his commanding staff
   rode briskly to the New York harbor side
and then embarking on the river craft
   crossed to the Brooklyn shore to reach the Heights.

When General Washington looked on the field
   the left and center lines had both collapsed
and men were running toward the Brooklyn hill,
   chased by the shot and shell of cannon blasts.

And General Stirling and his brave brigade
   were holding ground on the Gowanus line
while fighting back each charge the Hessians made
   while Howe was bearing down from the blind side.

And Stirling sent a company of men
   to guard the line of the brigade's retreat
then they saw British forces pouring in
   and setting up a line of batteries.

Then suddenly the cannons opened up
   and iron balls were smashing through the ranks
and canisters sent fiery hot grape shot
   that mutilated men in shredding pain.

The soldiers were surrounded on three sides
   and backed up to a marsh and flooded creek
and some men formed a final desperate line
   to try to cover others in retreat.

Composed and stoic General Washington
   was screaming horror silently inside
while witnessing the murder of the men
   who were completely cut off in the fight.

Some men could swim but many others drowned
   and floating bodies filled the water way
and in broad swaths the soldiers were cut down
   as the Gowanus Creek flowed blood that day.

Chapter 17

Saving the Continental Army
August 28–30, 1776

More reinforcements moved to Brooklyn Heights
    to keep the crucial battery secure.
Without high ground along the river's edge
    they could not hold position at New York.

The British began digging in their lines
    and August 28 they were entrenched
while redcoat ranks continued to arrive
    with thousands upon thousands pitching tents.

Some parties of the riflemen deployed
    to venture far outside the battlements
to keep the British infantry annoyed
    with talents of their long range marksmanship.

The redcoats lunged at groups of riflemen
    who sent pinpoints of shot into their lines
but did not charge the works with an offense
    so riflemen kept prowling the hillside.

Through morning heavy clouds on the horizon
    rolled in to darken the bright summer sky
and Patriots could see the British forming
    a body of redcoats to charge the Heights.

A heavy rain began to thunder down
    with signal guns and drumming of alarm
and as torrential rains dumped from the clouds
    the Patriots were posting with their arms.

As soldiers kept their post in soaking rain
    some were concerned their flintlocks would not fire
and if they had to face assaulting waves
    they wanted to make sure that they could fight.

So later in the afternoon some men
    fired muskets to ensure their guns weren't fouled
and many others started firing then
    as the high strung defensive lines unwound.

Then for some hours the soldiers lobbed potshots
    at British soldiers camped far out of range
and some thought redcoats mounted an assault
    through the blind curtain of the pouring rain.

The officers and sergeants scrambled round
    to clear up the confusion in the ranks
and in the evening soldiers settled down,
    exposed to storms all night without a break.

By morning trenches almost overflowed
    as heavy rain continued steadily
and ammunition on the men was soaked
    while they were stuck in muddy pools waist deep.

The night before the British had advanced
    and within half a mile entrenched more works
and set below in sprawling British camps
    was twice the number of the Army's force.

The Congress had expected Washington
    to keep New York out of the Brit's control
while managing the Army for defense
    but pinned down he would probably lose both.

Fort Washington and Lee were set upstream
    to keep the Hudson River under guard.
They did not have a choice but to retreat.
    Without the Army they would lose the war.

The General issued orders for the men
    to hold their fire both in and out of lines.
They could not shoot except in their defense
    or they would have to stand Court Martial trials.

Then Washington assigned some trusted squads
    to make sure each bateau had been prepared
to move at nightfall from the harbor's docks
    and meet the Army at the ferry's pier.

10,000 soldiers were at Brooklyn Heights
    and they had many wounded and infirmed.
They had to move in the short hours of night
    and Washington would not leave any men.

At dusk the soldiers were set to parade
    and gathered up the baggage that they had
then quietly lined up and slipped away
    to orderly embark on river flats.

And they dismounted the artillery
    and hauled the heavy metal of the guns
down from the Heights on steep roads quietly
    and carried cross the river countless tons.

George Washington stood on the Brooklyn shore
    and watched the careful loading of the troops.
He had declined suggestions he should board.
    He would not leave till every man was through.

And early in the morning General Howe
    was viewing with his glass the distant lines
to gloat upon the Patriots pinned down
    but saw no movement to his stunned surprise.

The British soldiers cautiously advanced
    expecting sudden opposition fire
but marched without event up to the trench
    then peered into the muddy, empty line.

Then rushing to the overlooking bluff
    that stood above the river and the bay
they saw the Patriots were shoving off
    as the last boat of soldiers was away.

Chapter 18

The Keenness of the Edge
September 11, 1776

After the tragic battle of Long Island
    the British had a set of terms for peace
and sent a message to arrange a meeting
    with Congress members of the colonies.

At Philadelphia three delegates
    were chosen to be the ambassadors
— Ben Franklin and then Edward Rutledge with
    John Adams set to travel to New York.

Arriving the 11th of September
    they met their rendezvous along the shore
with a small barge that carried British soldiers
    who stiffly stood under a truce of war.

The delegates then met an officer
    who said he had been sent as volunteer
to wait on shore as ransomed prisoner
    until the delegates' secure return.

The delegates realized the mortal risk
    of which they were endangering their lives.
King George III condemned the colonists
    and vowed to crush them for rebellious crimes.

Yet Adams knew they could act decently
    and spoke with the two other delegates,
then all three men wholeheartedly agreed
    they could expect a civil conference.

So as the officer had given charge
    to the discretion of the delegates,
they did not keep him as a prisoner
    but took him with them to the British camp.

They rode to Staten Island on the barge
    and met Lord Howe the British admiral
— the brother of the General Howe in charge
    of Britain's army troops of regulars.

As they had brought with them the officer
    sent as a ransom for the delegates,
the good faith gesture was received in turn
    as a clear sign of mutual respect.

Then they were led between the lines of guards
    of a large company of grenadiers
who snapped to orders while presenting arms
    before the passing group of visitors.

Then in the quarters billeted for Howe
    they sat officially for a cold meal
and quietly admitted the profound
    while stiffly moving through formalities.

After they had observed the formal meal,
    after the table had been neatly cleared,
Lord Howe spoke of his brother who was killed
    in the French War that lasted 7 years.

He held a love for the Americans
    especially the people of New England
who had devoted a stone monument
    to honor services of his past brother.

Then on behalf of King and Parliament
   he could present a treaty for their peace
and reconcile their hostile differences
   and offer pardons for the colonies.

Then Edward Rutledge pointed out the fact
   — there was a declaration that was made.
The colonies agreed to a compact
   for liberty as the United States.

The People had united to be free.
   There is no pardon that embraced submission.
They would not sign a treaty for the peace
   that did not recognize their independence.

Then Howe said that he lacked authority
   to recognize what Rutledge was insisting.
The independence of the colonies
   was not in the proposal he was given.

Then Adams mentioned the Suppression Act
   where they lost the protection of the Crown.
The King himself made independence fact
   by stating colonies were on their own.

Then Franklin said that England would retain
   a friendly ally for prosperity
if England honored the United States
   instead of making them an enemy.

Then Howe brought the discussion to an end.
   They were requesting what he could not do
and he escorted the three Congressmen
   back to the barge manned by the British crew.

And as they were set to be on their way
    for a return to the New Jersey shore,
Lord Howe paused so he could sincerely say
    a soft confession in his solemn words.

And a profundity was then revealed
    when the three Congressmen hear Lord Howe utter,
"If America falls, I will feel it
    and lament it like the loss of a brother."

Then Dr. Franklin gave a thoughtful answer
    he hoped would give Lord Howe some consolation,
"My Lord, we will do our utmost endeavors
    to save your Lordship that mortification."

Chapter 19

Kips Bay and Hell's Gate
September 12-15, 1776

With British forces on the Brooklyn Heights
    and gunships in command of water ways,
the Army could be trapped upon the isle
    and then bombarded with a cannonade.

George Washington was poignantly aware
    how dangerous the setting had become.
The British could attack from anywhere
    with Patriots outnumbered two to one.

One quarter of the men were deathly ill
    with dysentery and dour infirmities
and they could feel the falling autumn chill
    and many lacked warm coats for winter's freeze.

The General ordered sick and wounded men
    to be evacuated from New York
and the surplus not needed for defense
    to be removed and guarded farther north.

They kept the cannons in the batteries
    that stood upon the shores near New York harbor
but hauled away the field artillery
    along with some detachments of the soldiers.

They kept an Army presence in the city
    to check marines from landing an offense
but steadily moved up Manhattan Island
    to set in a position at Kingsbridge.

Then British movements began to suggest
   a plan to land their forces at Kips Bay,
located on the river to the east
   near where Long Island Sound pours through Hell Gate.

The British were seen moving transport flats
   into Long Island up the Newtown Creek
and they were setting to make an attack
   nearby Kips Bay along East River's beach.

So Washington sent men to reinforce
   entrenchments that secured the area
and guard the roads for the withdrawing corps
   with a stalwart protective barrier.

Then lengthening their breastworks at the shore
   they saw a British frigate nudge upstream
with cannon muzzles peeking through port doors
   foreboding ominous hostilities.

Then with two pieces of artillery
   the Patriots had rapidly deployed
they set the cannons for a battery
   and waited for the frigate to approach.

The air began to move with a stiff breeze
   as orders for the crew were clearly yelled
and sailors hauled the lines with hollered heaves
   as the ship's slackened sails began to swell.

The Patriots positioned patiently
   with two 12 pounders loaded in the wait
and the militia stood in lines to see
   the frigate slowly sailing into range.

Then as the ship was slowly moving past
    and when the order had been yelled to fire
the two big guns recoiled with roaring blasts
    and blew two holes straight through the ship's broadside.

The gunning crews then moved to load again
    while the militia in the trenches cheered
and pivoted the guns so they could send
    another shot before the frigate cleared.

The frigate fired one cannon at the shore
    — a 6 pounder that flew above the men
and the bad aim of the ship's one report
    set off a squall of laughing cheers again.

Then after passing the militia's line
    the frigate anchored within view upriver
and soldiers wished they'd pass a second time
    to shatter the ship's ribs and beams in shivers.

The next day four more British ships approached,
    much larger than the frigate sent before
and all the rows of port doors had been closed
    and the four gunships anchored off the shore.

The ships were nearly within musket range
    and riflemen positioned by the works
to look out on the boats with careful aim
    for any targets that they could discern.

But the boat crews were keeping below deck
    and with the port doors closed there were no shots
that any of the marksmen could attempt
    then day came to an end with blinding dark.

September 15 at the crack of day
   3 British man-o'-wars approached New York
and thundered with the broadside cannonades
   bombarding batteries along the shore.

The soldiers who remained at New York's camp
   jumped to report to post with the alarm
in case the British made attempts to land
   upon a beach to storm the city port.

Then General Washington and his whole staff
   were galloping down the Manhattan isle
responding to the launch of an attack
   before they could move to the country side.

At Kips Bay though the British ships laid calm
   and the militia stood at their breastworks
and stared upon the British ships at dawn
   while in the distance cannons could be heard.

The port doors of the gunships remained closed.
   The crews of the four boats could not be seen.
They rode their anchors on the river flow
   but all four boats appeared to be asleep.

Then cross the river the bateaux appeared
   with redcoat cargo quilled with bayonets
and a long line of the boats became clear
   as they arrived behind the row of ships.

Each flat was hauling at least 50 men
   and 80 of them paddled up the stream
beyond the Patriot's entrenched defense
   to land 4000 veteran marines.

In time the group of flats formed in a line
    upriver from the row of British ships
and then the British ships returned to life
    with sounds resounding from the oaken ribs.

At 10 AM the sun was shining bright
    and as the ships' port doors were opened wide
at least 100 cannons nudged in sight
    and peaked their muzzles in the broad day light.

There was a yawning of a cliff edge pause
    while cranks were turning as the guns took aim
and then a signal cannon was set off
    and blew away the doors of hellfire's gate.

The wave of shock stripped off the leaves of trees
    and iron shot was pounding on the works
as the incoming from artillery
    was pummeling with force to move the earth.

And all the men were ducking in the ditch.
    The air was one long swath of iron shot.
If any soldier looked up from the trench
    then instantly his head was taken off.

Upstream the flats were aiming for the beach
    so the marines would land above the flank
then the militia panicked at the scene
    and men began to break away from ranks.

But then George Washington was near the fight
    as cannon balls were launching from the guns
and tried in earnest to reform the line
    but all the men had broken in a run.

Some regiments from camp were on the march
   as forces from New York were coming up
but with the line completely blown apart
   there was the threat that they would be cut off.

Chapter 20

A Narrow Escape
September 15, 1776

As the defenses at Kips Bay collapsed
   the Army faced a new catastrophe
— the camp beside New York would soon be trapped
   if British blocked the line of the retreat.

They had been exercising a withdrawal,
   removing the field pieces and supplies
and food and ammunition had been hauled
   up to the north end of Manhattan isle.

At camp some Army personnel remained
   and they would need to rapidly remove
or pressed between marines and cannonades
   they risked the loss of several thousand troops.

The General notified the camp's command,
   the situation was then desperate
— they must directly organize the men
   and march the soldiers to evacuate.

And Washington was watching the marines
   attempting to form on the riverside,
they seemed to struggle on the muddy beach
   and fought against the ebbing of the tide.

He saw exactly how he could adjust
   his soldiers to keep the marines at bay
but at that point it made no difference
   — the whole militia force had run away.

The British force was floundering on shore
    and even though the cannonade was hot,
if Washington had a well-tempered force
    the landing on the shore could have been stopped.

He realized he could not rely upon
    militia men to hold a firm position.
They could defend their families and town
    but armies needed regular enlistments.

The Army could not beat the navy ships
    with transports and support near water lines.
The General had to use the continent
    and move the Army to the countryside.

The British force would not take long to form
    and Washington demanded urgency
to break the camp and get the men on course
    in the foreboding of emergency.

Then after a few hours the British troops
    were setting up entrenchments on the road
to block the Patriots before they moved
    then cannonade the camp with their gunboats.

But British officers were not aware
    another road ran near the Hudson edge
and regiments were marching unimpaired
    nearby the riverside much farther west.

Some cannons had been left at batteries
    and they were forced to leave stores of supplies
but the division of the infantry
    survived to guard their country in the fight.

And General Washington rode in the lead
    upon the roadway up Manhattan isle
to join the Continental Army's strength
    in a position at the Harlem Heights.

They vigorously built up battlements
    and dug entrenchments for a forward line
and all the soldiers worked with diligence
    — they knew the British would be close behind.

They had to back away from New York's port
    which proved an indefensible position
and then they could draw in the British force
    where they had more control of the conditions.

The hills would shield them from the navy guns
    as they secured a narrow neck of land
where British infantry would have to come
    and Washington would have direct command.

Chapter 21

The Battle of Harlem Heights
September 16, 1776

September 16 in the morning dew
    the British force was moving up their troops
with tapping drums and fifes that piped in tune
    with glinting bayonets and stomping boots.

George Washington had worked throughout the night
    and issued orders to the officers.
The soldiers would be strictly organized
    for a review in early morning hours.

Then at their posts along the battlements
    the soldiers stood in ranks of regiments
and Washington rode down the lines of men
    so they could feel their strength and unison.

The sergeants made each squad of men complete.
    Lieutenants organized squads in platoons.
The Captains then lined up the companies
    that snapped salutes with Washington's review.

And General Washington made sure the men
    were sharp and in good order for the day
as the brave Army of the Continent
    for the defense of the United States.

Far in advance of the entrenched front line
    the rangers and the riflemen had seen
in the clear day of the late morning light
    the columns of the British infantry.

The British had by far the larger force
   against the rangers and the riflemen
but Patriots had long range rifled bores
   and set to make a stand behind a fence.

The small detachment of the Patriots
   lined up behind the brush of a ravine
and waited till they had an open shot
   from their position set off distantly.

Then a long battle line of British men
   marched over a wide field to reach the edge
and began climbing over the rail fence
   in front of where the Patriots had set.

The Patriots had steadied their sharp aim
   and the commanding officer yelled, "Fire!"
and the ravine lit up with muzzle flames
   that let a volley of the bullets fly.

A number of the British soldiers fell
   and Patriots reloaded the next rounds.
The cause for liberty had rung the bell.
   They would not even think of backing down.

George Washington then heard the guns' report
   and rode in front of readied rows of men
that had been ordered in a solid corps
   and set the soldiers marching in advance.

The rangers and the riflemen held ground
   and poured the shot into the British ranks
and far from the protection of the Crown
   the British soldiers slowly backed away.

Withdrawing in the field they then reformed
    and stood beyond a normal musket's range
and hoped the Patriots would then be forced
    into the open ground to be repaid.

But Patriots then lined up at the fence
    delivering their deadly long range shot.
The British infantry had no defense
    and then more Patriots were coming up.

The British then retreated in the woods
    and tried reforming in the timbered stands
but Washington led a strong line of troops
    deploying orderly at his command.

The line of British troops kept marching in
    and Washington could sense the shifts of strength,
adjusting the positions of the men
    to counter everything the British sent.

For hours there was sustained intensity
    with a continuous, exploding roar
of musketry and field artillery
    in movements of the orchestrated war.

And General Washington and all his men
    were slowly beating British forces back
by feeling out the weak points of defense
    and thrusting forward with well-aimed attacks.

So inch by inch they drove for two long miles
    and sent more shot than British troops could bear,
then gunboats came in view off to the side
    and shrieking shells exploded in the air.

Then General Washington held the advance
   to stop from marching through the line of fire
of the artillery of British ships
   abruptly ending their momentous drive.

The Patriots lined up for a defense
   expecting British to form for attack
and waited to see what the King would send
   but British forces prudently held back.

The riflemen and rangers stayed out front
   as sentinels along the picket line
and the main force returned with Washington
   triumphantly to camp at Harlem Heights.

The next few days the fields remained at peace.
   The Patriots alertly kept a watch
but British troops were nowhere to be seen
   after they suffered the decisive loss.

Then on the 20th late in the night
   on the horizon was a glowing light
and tragically the Patriots realized
   that New York City was engulfed in fire.

Chapter 22

Direction and Decision
September – October 1776

Although New York had proved untenable
   there was a hope to block the river way
so British forces north of Canada
   and General Howe could not communicate.

Fort Washington on the Manhattan isle
   was built on rocky cliffs close to Kingsbridge
above the river with a line of fire
   yet the position came with certain risks.

If British forces moved in for a siege
   Fort Washington would promptly be cut off.
The fort had only two lines of retreat
   and those two lines could easily be blocked.

The General knew that they would need to move
   into the open country to the north
allowing the maneuvering of troops
   — they could not stay just to support the fort.

So Washington selected riflemen
   to guard the fort's stronghold and batteries
then if a siege was set, the garrison
   would give the Army time to send relief.

Then cross the river on New Jersey's banks
   George Washington sent men with General Greene
— three thousand and five hundred from the ranks
   to guard the Hudson River at Fort Lee.

The Army held the post at Harlem Heights
   in case the British marched up from New York
but Howe could use the ships at anytime
   and move his soldiers freely with transports.

Of course George Washington expected this
   and moved some regiments to landing sites
so if the British disembarked from ships
   the General would be promptly notified.

Defenses at the Heights were fortified
   and Patriots could crush the Brits' assaults
but competent commanders always try
   avoiding what the opposition wants.

But Washington could not march from the posts
   till Howe committed to another move.
He could not leave Fort Washington exposed
   for a direct advance of British troops.

The fort became more of a hindrance
   the General thought they should evacuate
but Congress had insisted to defend
   from British shipping on the waterway.

The Army was George Washington's command
   for national defense in time of war
to guard the People's interest and the land,
   but Continental Congress was in charge.

If life was simple there would be no need
   for a strong army to keep others safe,
but through the natural world's complexities
   the soldier's path is not the easy way.

The difficult is what most will avoid
    but difficulties make the way to honor
while strengthening in never ending toil
    through the development of polished soldiers.

So Washington set posts to block the ships
    and gave those posts the means for strong defense
and set positions for intelligence
    of when and where the British force was sent.

October 12 the British tried to land
    along Long Island Sound above New York
and Washington foresaw the British plan
    to circle round the Army at the north.

So General Washington prepared to move
    and march upland before the roads were blocked
and set up in position with the troops
    where he could choose the battles to be fought.

The Continental Army was the target
    the British force was aiming to destroy.
The General had to relocate the Army
    upland before the British could deploy.

White Plains, New York was in the countryside
    where many inland thoroughfares converged
and set above the British landing site
    where Washington could fight on his own terms.

October 22 they arrived
    and General Washington surveyed the land
for the position to lay down the line
    where they could make a strong defensive stand.

Then soldiers busily built battlements
    before the south side of the country town
while sending up almost 2000 men
    upon a westward hill called Chatterton.

Militia were positioned on the hill
    as they fought best behind a strong defense.
The General tried to keep them from the field
    and fortified their strength with veterans.

The hill's position was extremely strong
    and would be difficult to overtake.
The veterans would anchor with their brawn
    deterring what had happened at Kips Bay.

Then Washington sent horsemen down the roads
    to notify when British had appeared
and when the waves of infantry approached
    the place would have been carefully prepared.

Chapter 23

The Battle of White Plains
October 28, 1776

October 28 before White Plains
    the tension in the air was taut and tight
with redcoats marching from the country lanes
    and organizing into battle lines.

George Washington had all the men prepared
    with firm defenses dug into the field
and watched the British infantry appear
    as redcoats were continuing to build.

With General William Heath in charge at left
    and General Putnam leading at the right
George Washington positioned with his staff
    commanding from the center of the line.

The British staff was orchestrating troops
    and General Howe and his staff trotted round
with their field glasses distantly in view
    surveying the landscape about the town.

Across Bronx River the commanding hill
    had the attention of the British staff
who pointed out entrenchments that were built
    as General Howe was peering through his glass.

As British soldiers were arranged in place
    then Howe assigned an engineering team
to work for hours before noontime that day
    and build a bridge to span the river's stream.

And as the British force stood in array
    awaiting orders for a forward march
the engineers were hammering away
    while tapping tension of the looming charge.

Then redcoat regiments began to move
    in large formations marching to the right
behind the forward line of British troops
    with cannons and artillery supplies.

Then hauling heavy guns over the bridge
    they set 4000 soldiers to assault
the Patriot defenses on the ridge
    that Washington had earlier foresaw.

When the main force of British had advanced
    they marched across the open cautiously.
The Patriots had built a strong defense
    to face the waves of British infantry.

Each time the British tried to make a push
    to break the line at any focused point
the Patriots stood firm before the rush
    and measured volleys cut the British short.

There was no doubt the line was strong and firm
    as confidence was building in the troops
and with each order that the soldiers heard
    they moved in unison to execute.

Commanding the good order of defense
    George Washington was checking to the right
as British infantry launched an offense
    upon the hill across the riverside.

Although the hill had a much smaller force
    to battle off the British front assault
the prominence gave a superior
    position for the Patriots to guard.

The British had to climb up a steep slope
    with Patriots above at battlements
and to make sure that the defense would hold
    the General had inspected it himself.

Then he could see the smoke upon the hill.
    The trenches were lit up with musket fire
and Washington turned back to watch the field
    adjusting forces to shore up the line.

The next time Washington looked to the right
    he had to steady his beleaguered will
as he saw soldiers running in brisk flight
    retreating down the backside of the hill.

The British had not stormed the battlements.
    The General saw them firing from below.
And Patriots were holding the defense.
    The General saw their clouds of musket smoke.

But when the redcoats started to approach
    the men in the militia ran away
and straggled off, abandoning their posts
    while battle hardened veterans remained.

Then Washington was keeping a close eye
    on movement of the British front's attack
and hoped the veterans could hold the line
    although their numbers were reduced by half.

The valiant veterans put up a fight
    but the thin number of the guns decreased
and British slowly gained ground on the heights
    and forced the veterans into retreat.

Then British soldiers brought the cannons up
    where they could fire into the Army trenches
and forced the Continentals to adjust
    and form another line of their defenses.

Then under orders the front was removed
    and hurried to the other side of town
where officers began reforming troops
    to set the next entrenched position down.

They had to give up ground out of the range
    of British batteries set on the hill
but as the new defenses had been made
    the Patriots stood firm upon the field.

Then dug into the new defensive line
    they waited for the British to attack
but then the afternoon slipped into night
    and General Howe seemed to be holding back.

Chapter 24

The Thinning Ranks
October – November 1776

The next day British numbers had increased
  as redcoat ranks continued to arrive
and Patriots refrained from any sleep
  to fortify their new entrenchment lines.

The Patriots were braced for an assault,
  fully prepared to fight another day.
They managed to reform from the withdrawal
  and kept their order to coordinate.

Then Howe removed the cannons from the hill
  and ordered British forces to reform
and filed the regiments off of the field
  as they appeared to march back to New York.

The move could easily have been a trick
  to draw the Patriots from their defense.
The Continental Army was dug in
  and had begun to fight with confidence.

But Washington realized there was the threat
  that Howe had planned to siege Fort Washington
or cross into New Jersey's land instead
  with routes and roads into the continent.

They needed to protect the passage north
  to block the British force in Canada
but they could not leave a wide open door
  for Howe to march on Philadelphia.

So Washington was forced to make a choice
— he had to split the Army in two halves
and leave one guarding roads up to the north
   and then the other half would double back.

He left 6000 men with General Lee
   at Castle Hill some miles above White Plains.
Charles Lee would hold the roads defensively
   and wait to see if Howe turned back that way.

Then Washington would lead 5000 men
   to Peekskill where they'd cross on ferry boats
beyond the passage of the British ships
   then march back south along the other shore.

When they determined what Howe planned to do
   they'd move to reconsolidate the force
then press engagements with the British troops
   when the diverging halves had been rejoined.

George Washington could not place risky bets
   pursuing after Howe's withdrawing line.
A British trap could easily be set
   with shipping lanes converging to each side.

The British had an army twice the size
   of the whole Continental Army's corps.
If they chased Howe directly from behind
   they'd be surrounded by the Brit's transports.

They needed to support Fort Washington
   if General Howe designed to set a siege.
The fort had food and a strong garrison
   to hold up for a couple weeks at least.

So Washington crossed on the Hudson River
    to follow Howe upon the other shore.
It was a longer march for the brave soldiers
    amounting to a 65 mile tour.

And if Howe planned to march directly south
    for an attack on Philadelphia
then Washington could dig in on the route
    to shield the Continental Capital.

But with year's end they faced another crisis
    as the enlistment terms would shortly end
and Congress was withholding the enticements
    of bounties for the men to re-enlist.

The Congress was relying on militias
    to bolster Continental Army strength
but General Washington had been insisting
    along a different line of reasoning.

They were not just a group of colonies.
    They were united as a single nation.
The Congress had responsibility
    for the protection of the population.

They had declared the right to raise an Army
    and must enlist the soldiers for long term.
If Congress could maintain a standing Army
    they'd have a fighting force to win the war.

And Washington was watching in despair
    as soldiers slogged along the grueling march.
The ranks were terribly in disrepair
    and all the weary soldiers were half-starved.

Then in November temperatures had chilled
    and most the soldiers did not have warm coats
so many men were regularly ill
    with tattered shirts and pants in rain and cold.

Then many men had worn away their boots
    and since the Army had such meager means
they could not find replacements for the shoes
    and soldiers tied up rags on their bare feet.

Then through the frost through many freezing nights
    they lacked in tents and blankets for the men
and soldiers had another war to fight
    with the exposure to the elements.

And when the soldiers were supplied some food
    the bug infested bread might chip their teeth
and if they had something from off the hoof
    they'd pick the maggots from the char burnt beef.

And as the soldiers staggered down the path
    there was concern the Army might dissolve
and by the time they were in Hackensack
    one half the force already had been lost.

A message was received on the 16th
    that greeted Washington with shock and grief
— the fort had been surrendered in defeat
    on the 1st day that Howe had set the siege.

The fort contained almost 3000 men
    with food, supplies and the artillery
and everything was tossed into the wind
    the moment they arrived to give relief.

November 20 more news arrived
— 200 British transports had been launched
and they were landing on the riverside
above Fort Lee to make a ground assault.

From Staten Island British would embark
to march straight into Pennsylvania.
The Continentals had to cut them off
and guard the roads to Philadelphia.

The soldiers in Fort Lee's held garrison
evacuated with commander Greene
as British General Charles Cornwallis was
advancing with 10,000 infantry.

So Washington held conference with his staff
and issued orders to the Army troops
to break their camp so everyone could pack
— the Army must immediately move.

Chapter 25

The March through New Jersey
November – December 1776

The Army had diminished in its strength
   and weary soldiers had been wearing thin
and even with the garrison with Greene
   the General only had 5000 men.

A message was sent up to General Lee
   to notify him of the British plan
and his command was needed urgently
   to help oppose the threatening advance.

Then Washington directed the hard march
   and held the haggard Army all together,
maintaining rapid movement of the force
   to Newark where they camped in late November.

At Newark Washington reorganized
   and let the soldiers have a moment's rest
while trying to replenish their supplies
   from the supportive local populace.

The Army then absorbed another loss
   as some enlistment terms came to an end
— 2000 soldiers suddenly walked off,
   reducing numbers to 3000 men.

And as the situation fell apart
   George Washington held onto what he had
then leaving Newark they began to march
   with the rear guard set at the Army's back.

The rear guard stayed in Newark for some days
　　allowing ranks and files to cover ground
and as the Army safely was away
　　the 28th the guard packed up from town.

And after the rear guard had packed their gear
　　and organized to set off on a march,
they heard the redcoat infantry was near
　　as British forces were pursuing hard.

There is a river called the Raritan
　　beneath the Staten Island landing sites
where Washington thought they could make a stand
　　with hopes militias could bulk up their size.

But when George Washington rode up ahead
　　he saw the water level was too low,
the fords across the shallow river bed
　　placed no demands for bridges or for boats.

There were too many miles of waterfront
　　for Patriots to line up and defend.
The British could then target any spot
　　and Patriots would be spread out too thin.

Then the militia in proximity
　　was having trouble mustering the men
while they evacuated families,
　　they'd have to wait till later to join in.

So then the Army was compelled to bear
　　an ordered march another hundred miles
then crossed the river called the Delaware
　　and dug in on the Pennsylvania side.

The Delaware was deep enough to block
   the forward movement of a staged offense.
The British force would have to boat across
   and would be hampered by the hindrance.

Then Washington set out to find the boats
   the British could make use of as transports
and made sure all of them had been destroyed
   to keep the British held up at the shore.

Cornwallis marched up with 10,000 men
   — three times the number of the Patriots.
The river was the key to the defense
   to guard the Continental Capital.

Militias throughout Pennsylvania
   then mustered up 2000 soldiers more
and Congress held in Philadelphia
   was working to support the Army corps.

The means of Congress were in tight restraint.
   They lacked a solid specie currency.
For decades colonies were blocked in trade
   and gold and silver were a scarcity.

The Congress had to print out tender notes
   so the commercial trade kept circulating
but without vaults of silver and of gold
   the tender rapidly depreciated.

They had sent envoys of ambassadors
   soliciting some foreign governments
but they could only hope to gain support
   with prospects for the other's benefit.

Congress acknowledged General Washington
    and began offering 3 year enlistments
and then through treaties tried to garner funds
    to purchase more provisions and equipment.

While Congress worked on the administration
    the Army had to hold upon the field.
They had declared themselves a sovereign nation
    but had to guard what they had aimed to build.

The Army was outnumbered 3 to 1.
    The icy winds were blowing from the north.
The short days of December had begun
    with nights that freeze a body to the core.

Some thought the war impossible to win
    and said that independence was too tough
but soldiers at their posts would not give in,
    the soldiers at their posts would not give up.

One soldier who had marched down from Fort Lee
    strolled to his home in Philadelphia
and jotted down a brilliant summary
    to harden the resolve and stamina.

Then Thomas Paine returned on the 19th
    and passed out pamphlets in the bitter cold
with sense and purpose to their misery,
    he said, "These are the times that try men's souls."

Chapter 26

The Battle of Trenton
December 26, 1776

December 25 was very cold
    and ice was building on the Delaware.
The heavy clouds foretold of storms and snow
    and winds were buffeting with blustery air.

The Delaware had held Cornwallis back
    without a means to move across the water.
He could not organize for an attack
    with the impediment of the broad river.

So British had set in for winter quarters
    and spread out through New Jersey and New York
while placing garrisons at separate measures
    to hold the roadways with the British force.

The banks along the rolling Delaware
    extended dicey shelves of cloudy ice
and the strong current's flow would crack and tear
    large chunks that clacked and crashed while drifting by.

Across the river from the Patriots
    were 1500 Hessian infantry
positioned as a Trenton garrison
    with more support in close proximity.

For months the Army had been battered back
    and fell from the position at New York.
The General struggled to keep them intact
    to save the Continental fighting force.

But many people's confidence had waned
   and some began to doubt about success
with loss of hope the cause could not sustain
   for independence and self-governance.

Through winter British forces would regroup
   with blankets, coats and plentiful supplies.
If Patriots just sat the winter through
   the spirit of their liberty would die.

They were into the winter's hardened time
   and Washington knew well the challenges
but he would not surrender from the fight
   — the aim for independence was not dead.

Then in the harsh and weary winter night,
   while others rested, they would push ahead.
Their aim for freedom would remain alive
   as long as men would stand and fight for it.

The temperature was brutal through the day.
   The night would be much worse and miserable.
The Army soldiers were set to parade
   as Washington prepared for an assault.

One group would cross downstream at Burlington
   for a diversion on a garrison.
Another force would cross and then make ground
   at Trenton to secure a bridge at dawn.

The main force would be led by Washington
   to cross the river at McKonkey's Ferry,
then they would march 9 miles up to the town
   and the defenses would be swept and carried.

The main force would advance with the attack,
    the other would secure Assunpink Creek
and hold the bridge with their whole regiment
    to block the Hessian garrison's retreat.

Then at McKonkey's Ferry after dark
    the soldiers began working at the chore
of loading cannons on flat bottom barques
    they had to drag up on the solid shore.

They could not roll the cannons on the ice
    and risk the heavy metal plunging through,
then slipped while heaving for the boats to slide
    as the artillery was tough to move.

Then at the shelf at the collapsing ledge
    as cracking ice was breaking underneath,
they held the boat at the unstable edge
    to keep it upright in the rushing stream.

Their feet were stumbling, slipping icy stumps,
    their clothes were sopping dripping, drenched and soaked,
their hands were fumbling and completely numb
    with grueling labor in the freezing cold.

Yet still they all had to work carefully,
    completing difficulties quietly,
if guards detected them while laboring
    they'd all be shot before they crossed the stream.

Then in the water they fought chunks of ice
    that caught the current to capsize the boats
and they were pushing off to pass them by
    while navigating cross the river flow.

And when the first boats reached the other side
    wild thoughts were flashing through the soldiers' minds.
For all they knew, they'd meet some musket fire
    — a lot of labor for a chance to die.

But as they dragged the boats onto the shelf
    they listened carefully into the night
and there were no alarms or orders yelled
    and calm relief embraced them with delight.

And General Washington was standing firm
    as stormy skies were dropping snow and sleet
and without uttering a single word
    he gave assurance for their victory.

They set up guards at the perimeter
    while dragging boats onto the river side
and worked while taking care not to disturb
    a picket post and ruin the surprise.

At 3 AM they formed upon two roads
    with separate columns moving parallel
and 9 long miles to march through sleet and snow
    with cannons and the loads of shot and shell.

The General knew that they were running late.
    They would not reach the town before the dawn.
The Hessians would already be awake
    requiring they adjust what must be done.

The General told commanding officers
    of the necessity of a hard march
and not to stop to fire on outpost guards
    but drive straight through them in a running charge.

And as the columns were approaching town
    the Hessian guards fired off some rounds of shot
but did not load again and turned around
    to run because the columns would not stop.

The General saw 3 Hessian regiments
    that rushed to line up on a Trenton street
then ordered for the column on the left
    to march around to cut off their retreat.

Then Colonel Knox lined up artillery
    upon the roads that headed to New York
and were positioned to sweep clean the streets
    as the 3 regiments turned to the north.

The Hessian regiments then recognized
    they ran straight toward the open cannons' mouths
and most veered to an orchard at the side
    and others turned around and ran back south.

Inside the orchard they tried to reform
    to charge and break the Continental line
but then surrendered and laid down their arms
    when they saw Patriots on every side.

Regretfully the other two divisions
    had been unable to traverse the river
and were not set in their assigned positions
    or they'd have captured every Hessian soldier.

They had not captured the whole garrison,
    500 of the Hessian force escaped
but then 900 were made prisoners
    and the brave Patriots had won the day.

1777

Chapter 27

Staying a Step Ahead
January 2, 1777

On January 2 the next year
   Cornwallis brought the British back in force
to trounce and spoil the Patriot's good cheer
   from victory at Trenton days before.

Cornwallis called the troops from winter quarters
   and gathered the detachments in a march
to drive the Patriots into the river
   with their drawn bayonets in a fierce charge.

That morning skirmish fire popped in the air
   a few miles north of Trenton on Post Road
with halting shots upon the avant-garde
   reporting British forces that approached.

George Washington made sure they were prepared.
   He knew Cornwallis would retaliate
to damage the American repair
   of confidence in the United States.

They set up batteries outside of town
   with cannons they had previously seized
and lined up in entrenchments they laid down
   above the slope across Assunpink Creek.

The outposts of the picket line came in
   with an assessment of the British corps.
They'd need to brace to set a strong defense.
   Cornwallis had assembled a large force.

George Washington had General Greene at left
    next to the southbound road to Burlington,
set in position to secure the bridge
    with regiments of Army Patriots.

Then General John Cadwalader was center
    with Philadelphia militia ranks
and to the right were men with General Mercer
    prepared to pivot and deny the flank.

At noon the British force was coming up
    and marched into position cross the creek
with 7000 soldiers in the troops
    and limbered lines of their artillery.

Opposing lines were outside musket range,
    the water in the creek too deep to ford,
so both sides' batteries came into play
    with the bombardment of each other's corps.

The guns were thundering on either side
    and bombs exploded over soldiers' heads
then British began forming into lines,
    amassing personnel close to the bridge.

Then General Greene reorganized his men
    while British cannons turned to aim his way
and as the Army shored up their defense
    the British cannons fired to find the range.

Then there was a short softening and pause
    and guns were loaded by the British crews
that tamped the powder charges, wads and shot
    and waited for the orders to issue.

The Patriots were crouched down in their lines
   in the brief moment of the lulling calm
while redcoat infantry amassed in sight
   across the bridge upon the open road.

The British soldiers were formed into ranks
   and infantry and grenadiers were set
to plunge into the lines of Patriots
   with rushing waves of lowered bayonets.

Then they heard the command yelled out to "Fire!"
   ride on the surge of an explosive shock
and screaming chunks of iron filled the air
   with the bombardment of both shell and shot.

And General Greene was yelling through the roar
   for his brave men to keep their nerve and wait
for forward movement of the British force
   under the cover of the cannonade.

Then as the British infantry deployed
   they saw no Patriots at the breastworks
as cannon shot was pounding on the soil
   and screeching bombs exploded shrapnel bursts.

The British infantry marched on the bridge
   within the range of flintlock musket shot,
then suddenly the redcoat soldiers flinched
   as the front line of Patriots stood up.

The hammers of the muskets had been cocked
   and steadily the Patriots took aim
and then a wall of fire from the flintlocks
   sent bullets cutting through the British ranks.

The Patriots kept pouring in the fire
    as soldiers loaded, aimed and fired again
and then the British force had to retire
    against the molten river of hot lead.

After the British forces were denied
    the sun had set and daylight quickly dimmed
and operations halted for the night
    and then the next day would start up again.

The Patriots had dug a strong defense
    but they were in a tight predicament.
The Delaware was blocking them from camp
    and rations were diminishing again.

The British would make a new strategy
    and the next day the fighting would resume
but Washington had no intent to see
    what General Charles Cornwallis planned to do.

Chapter 28

The Battle of Princeton
January 3, 1777

On January 3 at 2 AM
    the Patriots were gathering their gear
and working earnestly to break down camp
    to leave the British soldiers unaware.

400 Continental soldiers stayed
    to keep the several hundred campfires lit
then improvised for a theatric play
    like they were reinforcing battlements.

Then the divisions lined up on the road
    to gather in formations in the dark
and with commanding orders whispered low
    they started in an orderly night march.

The soldiers did not march along the river
    to safely cross upon the Delaware.
Their march was heading further in New Jersey
    although they did not know exactly where.

They marched for 16 miles through the cold night
    so the advance was crossing Stony Creek
just as the sky was brightening with light
    then filed in ranks to Princeton earnestly.

Not waiting for Cornwallis' next move
    George Washington took the initiative
with what no one expected him to do
    and strike behind Cornwallis' offense.

So as Cornwallis had built up his force
    at Trenton to attack the Patriots,
he'd weakened the defense for his support
    that General Washington then aimed to cut.

Approaching Princeton Washington had planned
    to capture the detachment's garrison
and sent Cadwalader and Sullivan
    with their divisions to surround the town.

Then General Mercer was directly sent
    to set up guard upon the Trenton Road
and hold the ground with his small regiment
    if the returning British force approached.

Yet war has ways that seldom follow plans
    with constant changes as with life and weather
and fortune spins the wheel of circumstance
    to make selections from the unexpected.

As turns, the Princeton garrison deployed
    a force consisting of 800 men
and they were marching off to reinforce
    Cornwallis for the coming day's offense.

As the redcoats were marching out of town
    they saw the Patriots at Stony Creek
and set in a position on the grounds
    outside of Princeton surreptitiously.

Hugh Mercer led 350 men
    to a location at the roadway pass
with the intent to set up a defense
    but soon discovered they had sprung a trap.

Within the narrow range of 50 yards
    the British soldiers stood up from their cover
and hundreds of the muskets were discharged
    and ripped into the Continental soldiers.

Hugh Mercer ordered the return of fire
    and the small regiment tried holding ground
but then the British formed into a line
    and charged with their sharp bayonets held out.

The Patriots did not have bayonets,
    yet stood to try to fight the British back
and redcoat soldiers yelled in the onset
    as the whole line came rushing in attack.

Hugh Mercer bravely fought with his sharp sword
    and soldiers swung their guns like heavy clubs
but far outnumbered by the British force
    the tiny regiment was broken up.

The shattered regiment had to retreat
    to form another line for a defense
and after battling courageously
    Hugh Mercer lay amongst the fallen men.

The Patriots reformed in firing lines
    to check the British regiments' advance
and then Cadwalader marched double time
    with Philadelphia militia men.

Cadwalader then formed upon the field
    and moved a column of militia in
for an advance on ground the British held
    between two hills along a line of fence.

But the position proved to be too strong
   and British set 8 cannons on a hill
and they were firing canisters and bombs
   to make the column lurch at a standstill.

The British line kept up a steady fire
   and with the British battery in play
Cadwalader lost the momentous drive
   and the militia had to back away.

Then set beyond the reach of musket range
   the two opposing lines stood at a hold
and looking out into the open day
   they heard the gallop of a horse approach.

Then General Washington raced to the front
   and on his grey rode out before the men
and in the light of the bright winter sun
   he rallied and reformed the regiments.

Like building up a tide prepared to roll
   George Washington lined up the men to march
and yelled, "Parade with us my brave fellows!"
   and as he shouted, led the forward charge.

And like a thrusting sword plunged to the hilt
   with shouts and hollers surging in advance
the Patriots were storming cross the field
   and British soldiers dropped their guns and ran.

When General Washington rode back in town
   200 British from the garrison
had been surrounded in Nassau Court House
   by the division led by Sullivan.

The British soldiers certainly were caught
　　yet still insensibly would not give up.
Then a field piece was brought with solid shot
　　by Captain Alexander Hamilton.

After they blew two holes straight through the walls
　　the Patriots prepared to storm inside
but then the charge came to a sudden halt
　　as a white flag began to wave in sight.

The British baggage was strewn out in scores
　　with guns and gear and the artillery
and Patriots collected British stores
　　for which the soldiers were in desperate need.

Soon after Patriots marched out of town
　　Cornwallis and his soldiers kept a course
and rushed through Princeton without slowing down
　　while rapidly retreating to New York.

Then Continentals moved to Morristown
　　to take up winter quarters till the spring.
Since leaving Boston they were beaten down
　　but ended the campaign with victories.

Chapter 29

Burgoyne's Plan
June – July 1777

The British General Burgoyne had a plan
  to severe the United States in half
with British troops that moved from Canada
  on Lake Champlain and northern mountain paths.

He also set another British party
  from Lake Ontario to travel east
and march along the Mohawk River valley
  to meet with Burgoyne north of Albany.

Then joining forces at the Hudson River
  they would communicate with General Howe
and seize complete control upon the water
  to cleave the colonies with one sharp blow.

And Burgoyne hired more German mercenaries
  along with several hundred tribal scouts
and then recruited ranks of local Tories
  in isolated settlements he found.

In June John Burgoyne launched a sorted fleet
  on Lake Champlain to move 8000 soldiers
to Fort Ticonderoga for a siege
  and then continue to the Hudson River.

General Arthur St. Clair was then commanding
  two thousand and five hundred Patriots
who served to man the fort that was defending
  the access of the passage from the north.

The fort was very strong upon the lake
    but was surrounded by some hilly peaks
and Patriots had to evacuate
    when British built up hilltop batteries.

And as the Patriots marched in retreat
    the Hessians caught a trailing regiment
and Patriots were trounced in a defeat
    at an encampment set near Hubbardton.

Then Burgoyne tried to hack through the dense woods
    while Patriots annoyed and caused distress
by felling trees that blocked the British troops
    while sniping from the boundless wilderness.

And complicating Burgoyne's passage through
    with means they had to frustrate and perturb,
the Patriots arranged to rendezvous
    and gather up again at Manchester.

For weeks the British struggled through the bush
    and were relieved to reach the Hudson River
then found a note a knife stuck to a post
    that said, "Thus far thou shalt go and no further."

Chapter 30

Fort Stanwix
August 1-5, 1777

Fort Stanwix stood in the deep wilderness
   upon the portage between two spillways
near Mohawk River's lofty fountainhead
   and Wood Creek toward Ontario's great lake.

On August 1 the fort received supplies
   with ample food for 700 men
that would hold up for 6 weeks and provide
   the sustenance for Patriot defense.

As it turns out this was a very rare
   fortuitous event for Patriots
as the next day a British force appeared
   and the supplies had been a stroke of luck.

The British Colonel Barry St. Leger
   had led 800 British regulars
who marched up from Ontario's great lake
   with Tories, scouts and some Canadians.

Arriving on the rugged Wood Creek road
   the British soldiers lined up in broad ranks
for a review and military show
   safely beyond Fort Stanwix's cannon range.

The redcoat regulars marched in sharp files
   and moved precisely in coordination
and rolled out their field pieces in a line
   to threaten Stanwix with intimidation.

The center stood with redcoat regiments
  with cannons and their crews lined up in front.
On either side were scouts and Tory men
  that far outnumbered the fort's garrison.

Then St. Leger was trotting in review
  inspecting the arrangement of the corps
and sent a message with a flag of truce
  requesting the surrender of the fort.

The fort's commander Peter Gansevoort
  received the note then thoughtfully perused
the courtesy of St. Leger's kind words
  and then politely said he must refuse.

With the response the Colonel then appeared
  to make a gesture of indignity,
incredulous the Patriots would jeer
  at Britain's vast superiority.

So St. Leger commanded cannons up
  and British wheeled their field guns into range
and after gunners loaded solid shot
  the British crews stepped back to post and wait.

Then St. Leger gave orders to his second
  who trotted to the British battery
and then delivering command's directions
  spoke with the Captain of the company.

The second promptly trotted to return
  back to the station at the Colonel's side
and then out loud the Captain could be heard
  to order a coordinated fire.

There was a fierce explosion from the guns
  and solid shot came pounding on the walls
and Patriots had heard and felt the thumps
  but Fort Stanwix withstood the cannonballs.

The British only carried 4 pound shot
  that struck the fort but hardly made a dent
then on the ground the cannonballs had plopped
  as harmless as a game of bowling pins.

Realizing that the walls could not be breached
  and infantry could not make an assault
the British Colonel ordered for a siege
  to wait till Patriot supplies ran out.

Yet St. Leger had planned to rendezvous
  with Burgoyne in the Hudson River valley.
Still he could not march past Fort Stanwix's troops
  as Patriots could easily surround him.

So British regulars were sent to work
  at clearing Wood Creek's road for more supplies.
Then St. Leger set posts around the fort,
  positioning a tight containment line.

Then Colonel Peter Gansevoort took note
  at British regulars that marched away
for the communication on the road
  that led back to Ontario's great lake.

The British kept a camp close to the road
  but had to spread their total force out thin
to keep the fort locked in the siege's hold
  so Patriots could not bring soldiers in.

Two days before when British had arrived
   a message had been sent by Gansevoort
so the militia would be notified
   they needed reinforcements at the fort.

So 20 miles downstream the Mohawk River
   the prompt militia mustered at Fort Dayton
and led by Colonel Nicolas Herkimer
   800 soldiers marched the 5th of August.

Encumbered by 400 ox drawn carts,
   negotiating difficult terrain
the Patriots pressed on the urgent march
   and travelled for 10 miles on the first day.

The road was on a shelf above the river
   with climbing slopes upon the other side
and the long path was nothing but a sliver
   that stretched the troops into a long, thin line.

Then back at Stanwix Colonel Gansevoort
   saw St. Leger was gathering a group
of scouts and Tories posted round the fort
   and sent them down the Mohawk River route.

The group consisted of 400 men
   and marched to stop the reinforcement troops
but Colonel Gansevoort was then pinned in
   and could not get a warning message through.

Chapter 31

Night Sortie
August 5-6, 1777

Since Gansevoort could not send out a warning
 he was considering another plan
that if the British saw their camp was burning
 then St. Leger would have to countermand.

He saw the British regulars march off
 and then a group of Tories with the scouts
and with his field glass checked for posts of guards
 the British would have picketed around.

Then from the lack of rising smoke from camps
 there were no soldiers tending to the fires
so St. Leger's set siege was undermanned
 with the detachments that he had assigned.

Then Gansevoort called Colonel M. Willet,
 the 2nd Officer in the command
and looking out from the fort's parapet
 he pointed out the gaps into the camp.

And they could see the tents and the supplies
 but there were no signs of activity
just lazy drifts of smoke from tiny fires
 at scattered guard posts that appeared asleep.

So they made note of the accessing paths
 in the large gaps between the picket posts
with the vacated sections of the camp
 where raiding parties could directly go.

As St. Leger expected a surrender
   the moment British forces had arrived,
he then thought that the Continental soldiers
   were only planning to stay safe inside.

So St. Leger sent soldiers for supplies
   and Tories with the scouts had been detached
and with no more than a thin picket line
   he left his camp wide open for attack.

Then Colonel Willet called two companies
   and ordered them to make the preparations
with flintlocks from Fort Stanwix's armory
   and torches for the secret operation.

One company would detail to set guard
   and block a counter from the British ranks.
The other would light torches and then spark
   a raging bonfire of the British camp.

That night the soldiers listened to instructions
   and the assignments for the tasks were made,
then soldiers checked their rounds of ammunition
   so everyone had a full cartridge case.

Then after midnight Willet took the lead
   as the two companies formed files outside
and squads in the advance moved quietly
   and captured guard posts sitting round the fires.

Then the first company set musket lines
   so as the fires in camp were being set,
once British soldiers had been organized
   the company would hold up a defense.

The other company ignited torches
   and rushing flames were flying through the night
and it began to look like early morning
   as the dark camp began to spark with fires.

They soon heard British shouting the alarm
   as sergeants roused the soldiers from their sleep
and then the drumming of the call to arms
   was sounding off for an emergency.

Then when the British rushed to fight the flames
   the line of Continentals marked their aim
and fired a volley to send them away
   until the camp was fully set ablaze.

Then Colonel Willet began calling out
   for all the men to rush back to the fort,
the camp was rising in a smoky cloud
   and would be only ashes by the morn.

Then Gansevoort could not resist the smile
   as he saw Continentals' silhouettes
who crossed the field with the background of fire
   while cheering with a glorious success.

Chapter 32

The Battle of Oriskany
August 6, 1777

Although the sortie was a great success
   it did not draw the group back to the camp
and so Herkimer and militia men
   continued marching straight into a trap.

With the steep slope of hills upon the left
   and then the river to the right below
the march was stretched along a narrow shelf
   and the militia soldiers were exposed.

At 10 AM about 6 miles from Stanwix
   the group was marching through a deep ravine
when they realized they were caught in an ambush
   while crossing over a steep mountain stream.

The slopes above and then the banks below
   were lined with scouts and Tories taking aim
and flintlock hammers snapped to fire the loads
   as musket muzzles began flashing flames.

The clouds of smoke kept puffing from the trees
   as each gun fired a deadly line of shot
that darted whistles through the air unseen
   to singe the knot where Patriots were caught.

The Patriots would try to duck for cover
   but if they found something to crouch behind
a searing pain would make them double over
   while hit by bullets from the other side.

And in the open soldiers tried to aim
    by searching for a target through the smoke
but scouts and Tories fired and ducked away
    behind the cover where they could reload.

And the militia men kept running up
    to reinforce the soldiers in advance
and formed into a circle as a group
    and without backing down they made a stand.

Herkimer worked to organize the men
    directing where to concentrate their fire
and with a hail of bullets coming in
    the Patriots were fiercely holding tight.

When one man fell, another filled the space
    to keep a steady fire in their defense.
With any gaps they might begin to cave
    and none of them was willing to give in.

After an hour there was a heavy storm
    but still the Patriots did not withdraw.
They kept their powder dry while they reformed
    and waited for the summer rain to stop.

Herkimer noticed a place on the slope
    where scouts and Tories had not fired a shot
and knew the space was open and exposed
    for them to concentrate a flash assault.

They needed to advance a forward thrust
    and move into a place of higher ground.
Then set to mount a counter from above
    they'd build up their momentum firing down.

Then when the rain let up, the soldiers charged
    and scrambled up the side of the ravine
and there was constant clatter from the arms
    while fighting through the woods from tree to tree.

By afternoon the enemy withdrew
    and the militia gathered to reform
but numbers had been drastically reduced
    as they had lost far more than half their force.

They left Fort Dayton with 800 men
    then only a few hundred still remained.
They would be slaughtered if attacked again
    and could not hold out for another day.

The road was strewn with injured, maimed and dead.
    Two hundred more were taken prisoner.
Another ambush could be set ahead.
    They needed to assemble more reserves.

Then the militia gathered injured soldiers
    and loaded up the dead upon their carts
and with their muskets born upon their shoulders
    the ranks withdrew on a dejected march.

Then at Fort Stanwix Gansevoort observed
    the scouts and Tories straggling back to camp
and they were leading many prisoners
    who had been taken from militia ranks.

But when the ambush party had returned
    the scouts and Tories seemed to be incensed
when they discovered that their camp was burned
    and they were arguing with British men.

Then St. Leger sent out another note
   demanding the surrender of the fort.
Communication downstream had been broke
   and Patriots would not be reinforced.

Still Colonel Peter Gansevoort refused.
   The fort was strong. They could hold the defense.
To break the siege though, they would need more troops
   so trusted Willet once again was sent.

Then after midnight Colonel Willet left,
   avoiding posted guards and sentinels
and only with a message and himself
   set on a mission that was critical.

Arriving at Fort Dayton the next morning
   the Colonel saw a glorious surprise
— the marching of the Continental Army
   was coming up as bright as new day light.

The Northern Army sent 900 men
   with General Arnold for the fort's relief
and Willet then saluted the command
   with reinforcements he was pleased to see.

When St. Leger received the information
   the Continental Army marched his way,
he saw forebodings of a devastation
   and ordered his men to move out that day.

When Arnold and the soldiers had arrived
   they had already satisfied their goal
as St. Leger and his force by that time
   were half way back to Lake Ontario.

Chapter 33

Burgoyne's Foraging Party
July – August 1777

John Burgoyne struggled through the wilderness
    and roughly cut a road from Lake Champlain
then at Fort Edwards paused for a redress,
    preparing to continue his campaign.

With the communications to the north
    they'd move the troops, equipment and provisions
and General Burgoyne had his soldiers work
    on building a boat bridge across the Hudson.

When the boat bridge was set across the river
    they'd have an open route to Albany
and with the road supporting the endeavor
    they'd rapidly deploy the infantry.

The scouts were sent in parties through the woods
    and raided tiny settlements around.
They'd set off from the lines of Burgoyne's troops
    and then returned to camp with grisly scalps.

Then one day there were cries of deep despair
    after an officer had recognized
one scalp was of a lady's flowing hair
    who was engaged to be the soldier's wife.

The lady, Miss McCrea, had turned 18
    and grew up in a humble, country house,
the beauty of a Tory family
    and loyal subject of the British Crown.

And these events were stirring up the people,
    increasing the support for Patriots
and volunteers joined in the Northern Army
    to battle for the independence cause.

The British then received some information
    of Patriot supplies near Bennington
and General Burgoyne planned an operation
    before construction of the bridge was done.

Among the mercenaries in the group
    that marched with Burgoyne south from Canada
were a few hundred cavalry dragoons
    who needed horses for effectiveness.

So Burgoyne organized 800 men
    with Tories, a few scouts and infantry
to join dragoons for raids and foraging
    to capture horses for the cavalry.

On August the 11 they set out
    at Batten Kill, a Hudson tributary,
under command of Colonel Frederick Baum
    of the dragoons and German mercenaries.

Their movement was impeded by 4 cannons
    and their precautionary pace was slow,
concerned the Patriots had set an ambush
    as they moved through the forest on the road.

Then August 13 nearby Sancoick's Mill
    200 locals wearing hunters' shirts
were lined up near the cover of a hill
    and raised their muskets for a volleyed burst.

Then when the men sent out a loud report
    the bullets flew with little damage done
and as if they were finished with the war,
    just as they came, they suddenly were gone.

So Colonel Baum sent his men in pursuit
    in hopes to capture some as prisoners
then gain some insight from the interviews
    for the locations of the hidden stores.

The scouts and infantry led the advance
    and Tories and dragoons were right behind
while marching down the road into the land
    to try to catch the locals in their flight.

The road was following a little creek
    with lining hills along the wagon path
and the surrounding woods were thick and deep
    and Colonel Baum began to sense a trap.

The Tories said they were near Bennington
    but Baum felt that they needed reinforcements
so he dispatched a message back to camp
    and as they waited, built up their defenses.

Upon a hill beside the country road
    Baum ordered a redoubt to be constructed
so cannons could command the lane's approach
    if the entrenched position was assaulted.

Then at the point the road crossed on the creek
    the men dug trenches and built up breastworks
and they were sweating in the summer heat
    to hold out till the group was reinforced.

And 4 miles down the road was Colonel Stark
    of fame from Bunker Hill at the stone wall
who mustered men from the Militia guard
    that stood near Bennington 1200 strong.

The 15th there were storms and heavy rain.
    Stark sent reconnaissance into the woods.
He knew that Burgoyne's troops were on the way
    but had been waiting longer than he should.

Then Stark gained information Burgoyne's men
    had stopped deep in the woods a few miles back
with a small force that dug in for defense,
    so Colonel Stark prepared for an attack.

Chapter 34

The Battle of Bennington
August 16, 1777

On August the 16th the storm had passed
   but then another front was moving in
as the two sides were headed for a storm
   with flashing lightning and tornado winds.

The men in the militia knew the land
   with hollows, hills and fields of the terrain
and Colonel Stark developed the day's plan
   for the most favored way to be engaged.

The British would be waiting at the road
   with dug entrenchments for a strong defense
and they would be prepared for Stark's approach
   upon the narrow lane with troops of men.

Stark had almost 2000 men by then,
   for the large force, the road was the best way,
but Stark was not about to march his men
   directly where the British guns were aimed.

So Colonel Stark had two groups organized
   — 300 soldiers were composing each,
and they would lead attacks from different sides
   to turn the British forces dizzily.

Each group would make an outstretched circuit loop
   and strike both flanks of the entrenched position
with Colonel Nichols from the northern route
   and Colonel Herrick from the south's direction.

Then Stark would wait to hear the guns' report
    when the initial contact had been made
and then he'd rush the road with the main force
    after the British force was turned away.

The two small groups left early in the morn
    to hike around the hills through the thick woods,
then Stark lined up 1200 in the corps
    to march the road along the mountain brook.

The two small groups each hiked a dozen miles
    while guided by the local residents
who hunted in these woods for all their lives
    and knew each feature of the rugged land.

They watched the shadows cast by the sunlight
    to coordinate from the converging sides
so both detachments struck at the same time
    to throw the British trenches out of line.

And Colonel Stark positioned on the road
    near where the British trenches had been dug
with ranks lined up beside the water's flow
    and listened closely for the starting gun.

The group with Colonel Nichols came in first
    in a long line that fanned out through the trees
and saw the redoubt on the hilltop perch
    and heard the sound of the crisp mountain creek.

As they approached the Germans spotted them
    and oddly one dragoon began to wave
and Nichols sent an order to his men
    to keep their pace and get in musket range.

And the militia men were quite surprised
    as the dragoons lined up to stare at them
while peering over the redoubt's north side
    instead of bracing firmly for defense.

The German Colonel Baum made a mistake
    and thought the men were Tory reinforcements
from the request he sent the prior day
    and the men had been sent by General Burgoyne.

The Patriots could see the puzzled faces
    when Colonel Nichols hollered, "Company!"
They had approached as close as 50 paces
    and halted with the Colonel's ordered lead.

Then the dragoons appeared in disarray
    when Colonel Nichols hollered, "Ready Arms!"
and as the Patriots were taking aim
    the Germans began jumping in alarm.

Directly after Nichols ordered, "Fire!"
    the line of muskets bellowed out a roar
and sent a searing volley into flight
    and the whole valley echoed the report.

The Germans were then firing in response
    and Nichol's men then stepped behind the trees
to cover while they loaded to take shots
    as Germans moved the light artillery.

Then soon dragoons were firing canisters
    in an attempt to scatter Nichol's men
as the redoubt's attention had been turned
    from covering the lower road's defense.

Then Colonel Herrick's group was coming up
    and fired upon the Tories from their flank
who scrambled in confusion to adjust
    and turned their focus from the wagon lane.

John Stark had ordered the men to advance
    and all the ranks were marching double time.
So far the day was going as he planned
    and they would soon be at the British line.

Stark heard the steady roll of musket fire
    that sounded heavy at both right and left
and Tories did not see Stark's forward line
    until the column was on top of them.

The line of infantry and Tories broke
    as hundreds of militia stormed their works
then scattered in retreat upon the road
    in a debacle like a dam had burst.

Then Stark turned the attention to the hill
    where the dragoons were holding the redoubt
and firing steadily upon the field
    behind the billowing gunpowder cloud.

The Patriots had a much larger force
    but the redoubt's defense was strong and firm
and Stark would lose too many of his corps
    before they hoped to overwhelm the berm.

So Stark had his men firing from the cover
    and darting back and forth between the trees.
The redoubt's powder could not last forever
    and the dragoons would then accept defeat.

Soon after, firing slowed from the redoubt
   and sputtered off into a total stop
then Stark demanded the dragoons come out
   or Patriots would charge with an assault.

Then the dragoons came storming down the hill,
   refusing to surrender on that day
and flashed their sabers of sharp tempered steel
   and tried to slash a way for an escape.

Yet in the glory of the final charge
   they were no match for the militia line
and the dragoons did not get very far
   against the steady aim of musket fire.

Then the militia cheered their victory
   and were so overwhelmed with the delight
they were surprised by marching infantry
   as British reinforcements then arrived.

Stark's men were scattered and disorganized
   and he was yelling for them to reform
and then the British set a firing line
   to riddle the confusion even more.

Each time the soldiers tried to form again
   the British volleys scattered them with shot
and the militia's day became unhinged
   — their victory began to fall apart.

Then Captain Warner with 300 men
   came marching down the road from Manchester
to form a core to build Stark's force again
   and brace the ship before it overturned.

Seth Warner's men set up a battle line
   that the militia men could gather in
and synchronizing in a rolling fire
   began to blast the British back again.

The British infantry fought stubbornly
   but soon they were completely overwhelmed
and as the infantry tried to retreat
   the Patriots were driving them pell-mell.

Then the militia chased them down the road
   until the sun on the horizon set
and so the foraging campaign had closed
   with Stark and the militia's grand success.

Chapter 35

Crossing the River
August – September 1777

With missing, casualties and prisoners
  the British lost at least 1000 men
and Burgoyne's party of the foragers
  was unsuccessful at a great expense.

Then August the 18th the bridge on boats
  had nearly reached completion on the Hudson
but with the storms the swollen river flow
  then swept away the engineers' construction.

Then scouts who had been hired to help the British
  were disappointed by the day's defeat,
deciding to return to their own village
  with ominous forebodings menacing.

The Tories began flitting from the ranks
  as Burgoyne's army seemed to fall apart.
The local royal loyals lost their faith
  and walked back home to families and farms.

Then many German mercenaries left,
  abandoning their shrinking regiments
preferring to survive the wilderness
  then seek employment with the hopelessness.

A message then arrived from Canada
  with news that St. Leger had to retreat.
Fort Stanwix had repulsed the group's advance
  and they returned downstream in sore defeat.

The message also mentioned General Howe
    who did not plan to meet Burgoyne's campaign,
embarking with his army to sail south
    for an attack on Philadelphia.

Then many cynics in the British camp
    said Howe had failed to reach into the country
and he commanded 30,000 men
    and Burgoyne only had 1/5th that number.

Yet Burgoyne still had redcoat regulars
    and a division of the mercenaries
and they would soldier forward on the march
    although a change of plan was necessary.

The camp would wait to gain the last supplies
    and draw in the detachments from the north,
then he would cut communication ties
    to strengthen and consolidate his force.

The engineers would build the bridge again
    and then his army would traverse the river,
soon after the campaign would recommence
    and they'd reach Albany for winter quarters.

September the boat bridge was made complete
    and posts along the north road had come in
then British forces crossed on the 13th
    and Burgoyne's men were on the march again.

The British made a very slow advance
    and moved no more than a few miles a day
and kept their battle columns at their camp
    while foraging provisions on the way.

At each new camp they dug defensive trenches
    and kept the 3 divisions in tight order
as they anticipated Continentals
    in the detachments of the Northern Army.

And Burgoyne hoped for a decisive battle
    that he could orchestrate upon the field
to win control of the whole Hudson Valley
    and demonstrate his military skill.

Downstream the Continentals had gained strength
    and volunteers arrived in companies
with triumphs of the recent victories
    as bells were ringing out for liberty.

But hearing of the loss of Lake Champlain
    when Fort Ticonderoga had been seized
the Continental Congress changed command
    of the positioned Northern Army's lead.

So General Gates was given the commission
    to guard the Hudson River waterway
with a priority upon the mission
    — defeating Burgoyne's army and campaign.

Chapter 36

The Battle of Freeman Farm
September 19, 1777

The site where General Gates set up was strong
   and sat upon the bluffs of Bemis Heights
and Burgoyne had to move along the road
   that travelled down the Hudson River side.

The British could not cut a different route
   no matter what John Burgoyne had preferred
and if he hoped to find a passage through
   he'd have to meet the Continentals first.

The British set their camp two miles away
   as Burgoyne tried to see what he could do
and General Gates could sense him hesitate
   while watching British movements in clear view.

Then Gates removed all sources of provisions
   while herding livestock into hidden glades.
If Burgoyne hoped to feed all his divisions
   they'd have to mow the fields and eat the hay.

Gates had a force of 7000 men
   and fortified to be invincible.
He wanted Burgoyne to launch an offense,
   the palisades were unassailable.

The British could not keep their camp forever.
   They needed food to keep their men alive.
They must attack, retreat or else surrender
   before they had exhausted their supplies.

But General Arnold — as subordinate,
   did not agree with Gates' choice to wait.
The British could bombard the Army's camp
   from hills upon the Continental's flank.

Arnold insisted they must take the field
   and shape a battle at the farms below
and not let Burgoyne seize upon the hills
   to push them from the bluffs that guard the road.

Gates leaned the force to weigh upon the right
   to cover both the road and river line
and needed Arnold to hold the left side
   and not break ranks to rush out for a fight.

Then on September 19 Gates could see
   the British columns lining up to march
on country lanes that ducked into the trees
   and Gates then ordered for a call to arms.

The British left was on the river road
   and then their center lined up for support,
which was where Gates expected them to go
   and where he had positioned his main force.

Than Arnold pointed out the British right
   on a wide march to meet the Army's left
and Gates felt it was but a feinting slight
   and thought the march of little consequence.

And Arnold asked permission to engage
   and Gates allowed him to send riflemen
but the division on the left must stay
   out of the skirmishing unless they're pressed.

So General Arnold rushed back to the left
    in the division under his command
and promptly dispatched Morgan's riflemen
    who knew the trails and contours of the land.

Then Arnold lined up his men for a tour
    — he felt they were more likely to be pressed
if they moved closer to the British force
    then they would have to fight in their defense.

Then Morgan's riflemen dashed up ahead
    and waited for the British to approach
and lining up along the forest edge
    they'd launch their deadly shot upon the road.

A musket's range was less than 80 yards
    but rifled barrels were more accurate
and expert riflemen could hit a mark
    at distances a half a mile away.

The soldiers at the British column's head
    could see the flash and distant puffs of smoke
and then there was the mortifying dread
    not knowing where the flying shot would go.

The rifled shot was coming from so far
    the British soldiers could not return fire
and with an iron will they held their march
    while soldiers toppled in their ranks and files.

And as the riflemen took careful aim
    they targeted the British officers,
then in confusion as command would change
    the units stumbled with the leaders hurt.

The British marched and kept an ordered pace
    without the space to turn or to adjust
and were confined within a wooden lane
    and marched directly toward the rifled guns.

And Arnold saw the fury of the fight
    not far ahead of the division's march
and ordered regiments in battle lines
    along the edge of fields at Freeman Farm.

The riflemen were half a mile away
    and clearly they were firmly holding ground
and then another column on parade
    was rapidly approaching Freeman's house.

The British center column had been turned
    and was deployed to march for reinforcement
and Arnold sent the riflemen the word
    to hold their fire and back into the forest.

Soon after the short message had been sent
    the firing cooled that held the wooded lane
as Morgan gathered up his riflemen
    to quickly draw them back out of the way.

The British right then tried to organize,
    relieved from deadly shots of riflemen
and there was a suspended ease of quiet
    contrasting the ferocious battle din.

Then as the British center crossed the field
    they marched in front of Arnold's batteries
and all the cannon bells began to peal
    to enfilade the British infantry.

Then Freeman Farm became a ring of fire
  and British forces scrambled in confusion
while burning with the heat from every side
  as hills reverberated the concussions.

The field was under Arnold's tight control
  and every time he saw the British move
he'd send them canisters and cannon balls
  to scatter everything they tried to do.

Then Arnold sent a message up to Gates
  requesting he deploy more regiments.
They had the chance to conquer the campaign
  and blow the British back to Canada.

And Gates was standing up on Bemis Heights
  and saw the smoke and heard the guns below
but still expected British on the right
  and ordered General Arnold to withdraw.

Then Arnold said he could not understand
  when Gates' message was sent to the front,
with all the noise of what he had at hand
  he'd hear the message after he had won.

Then from the heights Gates saw the British left
  march rapidly across to Freeman Farm
so Arnold's sole division was beset
  by all 3 columns of the British force.

All afternoon the men with Arnold fought.
  They did not yield or give an inch of ground.
For the whole day the field was fiercely hot
  and did not cool until the sun went down.

Then General Arnold ordered to pull back.
They could not hold the field without support.
The next day they would surely be attacked
after the British organized their force.

Chapter 37

The Foolish Fight Within
September – October 1777

Returning to the camp the soldiers cheered
   and Arnold was the center of attention
and then a messenger from staff appeared
   to summon General Arnold to a meeting.

Inside the tent of the command headquarters
   expressions of the officers were dour
and General Gates was waiting to see Arnold
   as the day's victory began to sour.

Gates thought that Arnold was too arrogant,
   performing through the day audaciously
and faulted the impetuous advance
   where General Arnold acted recklessly.

Then Arnold said the riflemen engaged
   so far ahead he had to move the men
inside the operation's field of range
   and cover General Morgan with defense.

The British center column then approached
   and would have murdered Morgan's riflemen
who took up a position on the road
   to block the British right from coming in.

Then Arnold said he had one column pinned
   and tore the British center all to pieces
and held the field with his division's grip
   and Burgoyne's army could have been defeated.

Then Gates remarked the British held the field
    and Arnold had to pull back with his corps.
Then Arnold said he would have won the field
    if he had properly been reinforced.

That instant General Gates jumped to his feet
    and said that Arnold could be court martialed
then ordered his command to be relieved
    and any more disruptions would stand trial.

Then Gates composed his summary report
    announcing how the British were repelled
and suffered decimation through their corps
    as Burgoyne's redcoat army almost fell.

And Gates said that he organized the men
    for the developments throughout the day
then countered British moving in advance
    and didn't mention General Arnold's name.

The day's report was sent direct to Congress
    when first it should have gone to Washington
and there were questions of the General's motives
    when he bypassed the Army's chief command.

Then General Gates reorganized his corps
    and relegated Arnold to the camp
to the administration of reports
    and gave another General his command.

The British forces occupied the field
    and built a strong redoubt at Freeman Farm
and then another on a nearby hill
    in General Burgoyne's careful forward march.

By moving up their base's main location
    they were positioned for a quick advance
in striking distance for their operations
    with stores of ammunition close at hand.

It is like water flowing to a dam
    with the persistent, incremental moves
till there's more pressure than the dam can stand
    and topples suddenly in a deluge.

So Burgoyne moved close to the Bemis Heights
    that Continental soldiers fortified
and tried to find where he could drive a spike
    to crack the dam and then debouch inside.

October 7 later in the morning
    the British moved 3 columns to their right
and sent some companies to reconnoiter
    for an attack upon the height's west side.

Then Gates had Morgan's riflemen deploy
    to meet the party moving through the woods
to keep the British companies embroiled
    then sounded the alarm for all the troops.

Chapter 38

The Battle of Bemis Heights
October 7, 1777

By 1 PM the British could be seen
  upon the wheat fields west of Freeman Farm
in battle lines with field artillery
  as an engagement had been set to start.

Two groups of riflemen moved up ahead
  and filed into the woods at double time
and split off to the right and to the left
  with the left wing division close behind.

Gates planned to set the marksmen in the trees
  to strike the Brit formations in the field,
so British opened up their batteries
  to cannonade the forest with their shells.

Then after a prolonged suppressive fire
  the British began marching to the woods
that stood between them and the Bemis Heights
  with rough terrain obstructed with thick brush.

The cannonade had made a lot of noise
  but proved of no effect as a deterrent
and Continental riflemen deployed
  had set in good position in the forest.

Then soon the right and left flanks of the British
  were taking a barrage of rifle shots
and in a wilderness of hot ballistics
  the ranks were thinning as the soldiers dropped.

The British center struggled to move up
    while fighting with the forest undergrowth
and blindly scuttled through the tangled scrubs
    as Patriots were set for their approach.

And as the center moved the flanks collapsed
    while drubbed by the relentless rifle fire
and with the outside columns falling back
    the center was exposed on either side.

The building roar of action at the front
    reached Arnold's tent and he began to fume
and with the temper of his boiling blood
    decided to suit up and join the troops.

He was directly disobeying orders
    as General Gates relieved him of command.
His former charge of Continental soldiers
    was reassigned with Gates' reprimand.

But while Gates stood and stared through his field glass
    upon the smoke that rose from woods below,
the roguish Arnold rode his stallion past
    and galloped down to the engagement's throes.

Then as he rode up to his old division
    the men responded with a strident cheer
and Arnold yelled if they would let him lead them
    and their approval sounded loud and clear.

And all the men were willfully inspired
    as Arnold led them forward in advance
and lining up a rolling wall of fire
    the British center did not have a chance.

So Arnold chose to act out on his own
   preferring his opinion over all
and sometimes the success of battles won
   will puff up hubris for a bitter fall.

With both flanks of the British falling back
   the riflemen attacked the center's sides
and Arnold signaled the men to attack
   and the division then began to drive.

The British soldiers stumbled in retreat
   colliding with each other through the brush
and Patriots pursued relentlessly
   with pounding volleys in the forward push.

The British soldiers staggered from the woods
   back to the cover of artillery
and then there was the shock as the ground shook
   as cannonballs were smashing through the trees.

The Continentals held at the field's edge
   and the two lines were out of musket range
but Morgan's riflemen were sending lead
   expressly in the British army ranks.

The British cannons furiously threw
   the canisters and shot incessantly
and riflemen were targeting the crews
   to silence cannons in the batteries.

The cannons' rolling fire began to slow
   as one by one the British gunners dropped
but then a British General boldly rode
   to organize the ranks for an assault.

Then as he rode before reforming lines
  there was a single rifleman's report
that sent a shot that whistled off in flight
  and then the officer dropped from his horse.

The British regiments then fell apart
  and began running back to their redoubts
then General Arnold signaled for a charge
  and Continentals stormed across the ground.

Then Arnold rode ahead to Freeman Farm
  where the main British redoubt had been built
and organized the soldiers to reform
  and gathered all their strength to rush the field.

The Continentals would need all their men
  to operate in ordered unity
to overwhelm the redoubt's firm defense
  and storm the works of British infantry.

The last retreating redcoats cleared the field
  and ran behind the wall of the redoubt
and notches in the British fort revealed
  a loaded line of open cannon mouths.

And Arnold lined the men up for the charge
  as the air settled with a heavy hush
and all the Continentals held their arms
  and waited for the sudden, open rush.

Then General Arnold hollered the command
  and all together the division ran
with muskets firmly clenched in their strong hands
  to overwhelm the British soldiers' stand.

The run was long across the open ground,
　　they only heard their steps and panting breath
and staring in the open cannons' mouths
　　there seemed to be naught else but quietness.

Then closing in upon the batteries
　　there was a flash of light beyond belief
and for so many soldiers instantly
　　that was the last thing they would ever see.

And grapeshot cut the soldiers into pieces
　　that scattered horribly across the field
and swaths of Continental companies
　　were blown apart with countless soldiers killed.

The standing soldiers could not hold the charge
　　and backed up as the crews worked to reload
and British set to fire more canisters
　　and pound the Patriots with heavy blows.

Then Patriots stretched the perimeter
　　to find another way for an approach
and as they circled round the British works
　　they saw the redoubt's backside was exposed.

So Morgan and his riflemen took aim
　　directly through the opening they found
and poured the shot into the huddled ranks
　　till British had abandoned the redoubt.

Then General Arnold signaled all the men
　　to move together on their building wave
and led the charge upon the next defense
　　and took a bullet in one of his legs.

The rush of soldiers flooded British works
    and pinned the redcoats down at Burgoyne's camp
while injured Arnold met a courier
    with Gates' message relayed through his staff.

The message ordered Arnold off the field.
    He was not authorized to leave his tent.
Then Arnold was moved to the hospital
    with a triumphant victory again.

The battle decimated Burgoyne's force
    and he tried organizing a retreat
with hopes to march his men back to the north
    and reach St. Lawrence and the British fleet.

But Continentals were in close pursuit
    and as the British ran out of supplies
John Burgoyne then surrendered sword and troops
    the 17th at Saratoga Heights.

Chapter 39

Commission and Commitment
June – September 1777

George Washington had been at Morristown
  when Burgoyne's army marched from Canada
and Washington was watching General Howe
  to see what the main British force had planned.

After White Plains the troops with General Lee
  had scattered and gone home the year before
after Charles Lee was captured separately
  relaxing at a house miles from his corps.

So early in the year George Washington
  watched Howe to see his movement from New York
and sent up Morgan and his riflemen
  supporting Gates' army to the north.

Detracting from the Army's central corps
  the General had detached his strongest troops
for the security of every point
  to block a British move from breaking through.

The British forces occupied New York
  but Continentals had the countryside
and holding England from acquiring more
  required integrity of the whole line.

George Washington held more than a position,
  he was the chief command of the defense,
not of himself, but of the nation's interest
  and this required a total selflessness.

July that year a note was intercepted
    where Howe told Burgoyne his strategic plan
and with the new intelligence detected
    then Putnam sent the note to Washington.

Howe wrote that he would use the British fleet
    and load up 18,000 of his men
and then embark upon the open sea
    on a campaign to launch a new offense.

Then General Howe wrote that he planned a feint
    to launch an operation farther south
then rapidly move to the Boston Bay
    supporting Burgoyne from New England towns.

The message seemed to be improbable
    with likelihood of a deceptive ruse
and General Washington was skeptical
    but there was still a chance it could be true.

When Washington marched from the Boston Bay
    he left the harbor with a strong defense
and British ships would suffer cannonades
    from the New Englanders' militia men.

If General Howe intended to support
    the British campaigned launched from Canada,
he'd use the Hudson River to move north
    not march across the mountain wilderness.

So General Washington stayed in position
    to operate both to the south and north
and see when General Howe made a commitment
    then move the Patriot's opposing force.

In late July the fleet had left the port
and sailed in open water to the east
and Washington then waited for reports
from where the British had returned from sea.

Soon word arrived from Pennsylvania
that British ships approached the Delaware
to make a threat on Philadelphia
and Washington began his movements there.

Then he received another urgent note
informing that the fleet returned to sea,
suggesting Howe was feinting with the boats
so Washington then held the troops to see.

The Royal fleet sailed up and down the coast
transporting British soldiers easily,
but Continentals had to march the roads
and Washington conserved their energy.

Mid-August Washington received the word
the fleet had sailed into the Chesapeake
and this news indicated and confirmed
the area that Howe was targeting.

The summer months were coming to an end.
It soon would be too late for a campaign.
In a few months the winter would set in
and Howe could not sail up to Boston Bay.

Then General Washington ordered divisions
to force a march to Philadelphia
and gather the detachments and militia
to guard the Continental Capital.

There was no doubt of the emergency
   and Howe had nearly twice as many soldiers
but all the hope of gaining liberty
   was being pushed with force to topple over.

The Continentals made a grueling march
   and soon arrived on August 25
with heavy cannons and their loaded carts
   for National and Capital defense.

Then General Washington reformed the ranks
   upon the British operation line
and dug entrenchments and then made their camp
   along the waters of the Brandywine.

Chapter 40

The Battle of Brandywine
September 11, 1777

George Washington had lined up the divisions
    to guard the fords that crossed the Brandywine
and soldiers fortified with the entrenchments
    extending on the river many miles.

A group had been detached with General Maxwell
    to watch the British march up from Elk River
and monitor the route the redcoats travelled
    while skirmishers annoyed Howe's new endeavor.

The Continentals set on the main road
    on Howe's invasive operation line
and Maxwell was confirming the approach
    ensuring the two armies would collide.

The heavy guns were hauled up on the knolls
    for a command of the broad open land
and soldiers earnestly dug in below
    to hold the ground along the river's strand.

The officers inspected the breastworks
    and the arrangements of the set defense
ensuring the positions were secure
    before the British infantry came in.

And Washington sent Hazen's regiment
    to post far to the right for miles upstream
so Howe could not march round the line's far end
    and come down on the flank clandestinely.

As an additional preventative
    the General posted horsemen on the roads
so information could be quickly sent
    if Howe intended a surprise approach.

Then in the early morning of the day
    on the 11th of the month September
the British force arrived on the roadway
    and cannons were unlimbered and positioned.

The British infantry formed battle lines
    and then the batteries began to play
to discompose the Continental side
    with the bombardments of a cannonade.

The British gave an overt demonstration
    that they were lining up for an offense
and Continentals braced in preparation
    on the main road to hold the line's defense.

Late morning General Washington was told
    there was another force upon a march
on an evasive circuit on the roads
    and crossed a ford beyond the Army's guard.

Then Washington gave orders to adjust,
    instructing the divisions on the right
to pivot toward the British coming up
    ensuring that their right flank was denied.

Before that single order was dispatched
    another horseman suddenly arrived
and said the other force was marching back
    and only feinted circling out wide.

George Washington then made a countermand.
    He could not move divisions from the fords.
With British forces marching back again
    they'd cross the stream with no opposing force.

Still Washington sent out more messengers
    to clear up the conflicting information.
He needed more assurance to confirm
    the soldiers were set in the best formation.

More horsemen from the cavalry returned
    and said there were no signs from the far right.
The British force would have been seen or heard
    if they already crossed the Brandywine.

Then 2 PM an urgent note arrived
    — the British were approaching the right flank
and there was no denying it this time
    with redcoats forming lines 3 miles away.

Then General Washington sent pressing orders
    for three divisions of the corps to move.
They had to reposition all the soldiers
    as the redcoats were marching into view.

3 miles away on top of Osborn Hill
    the British ranks were forming into lines
in preparation to march on the field
    to strike upon the side and from behind.

The leaders could not survey the terrain
    and improvised to space the line of men.
They simply found an elevated place
    and tried to patch together a defense.

And as the Continentals scrambled round
   the British started coming down the slope
and Continentals had not found the ground
   where they could organize and try to hold.

The redcoat lines were marching cross the plane
   and Continentals fell into a front
to form a line in a haphazard way
   as British infantry was coming up.

And Washington called up one more division
   to quickly move away from the main road
and reinforce the others in position
   to brace against the impact of the blow.

Then as the British force was drawing close,
   before the reinforcements had arrived,
one General double checked his ranks and rows
   and saw his soldiers were far out of line.

They were offline by several hundred yards
   and they had left the front with a huge gap
and he began to holler at his charge
   to move before they're struck by the attack.

Horrifically by then it was too late.
   The British were directly on their heels
and the division could not form their ranks
   and they were quickly driven cross the field.

From there the line began to tear apart.
   The other two divisions could not hold
while trying to repel a forward charge
   with a whole flank torn open and exposed.

When reinforcements rushed into the fight
    the British victory was near complete
and they could only set defensive lines
    to cover for an orderly retreat.

And when the reinforcements had detached
    the British also charged on the main road
and the additional line of attack
    caused the entire position to implode.

The Continentals pulled back in retreat
    and Washington withdrew them in good order
and they would have to recollect their strength
    at Chester to reorganize the soldiers.

Chapter 41

Beaten yet Undefeated
September – October 1777

After the Patriots reformed at Chester
   the Continentals set to march again
to block the British army from advancing
   by holding Philadelphia's defense.

The Continentals suffered casualties
   and lost 1000 men at Brandywine
with captured soldiers, deaths and injuries
   while fighting valiantly upon the line.

The Army as a whole made a retreat
   as many lives were lost upon the front
and while the Continentals gathered strength
   George Washington reported to Hancock.

He told the President what had gone wrong
   with the confusion in communications
and took accountability of loss
   and was preparing for the next engagement.

The Continental Army was intact
   and they were dedicated to the cause
and Britain would persist in their attacks
   till a decisive battle had been fought.

The gift of Liberty would be preserved
   in the devoted spirit of the People.
The Nation's independence would endure.
   The States united could not be defeated.

For several days the two opposing armies
   maneuvered through the Pennsylvania roads
till on the 16th nearby Warren's Tavern
   their columns once again made an approach.

The Army's battle lines began to spread
   and skirmishers began to sputter fire
while overhead the heavy thunderheads
   were throwing lightning bolts down from the sky.

With the explosion of each lightning flash
   a crack would splinter from the darkened clouds
and then precipitating with the crash
   torrential rain began to thunder down.

The pressure building up the heat of war
   began to slip upon the muddy slopes
and soppy water drenched each loaded charge
   and powder soaked with rain would not explode.

George Washington knew his men's poor equipment
   would suffer damage in the wet conditions
and as their cartridge boxes were defective
   the soldiers' ammunition would be ruined.

So Washington gave orders to withdraw,
   their ammunition was completely drenched.
If Continentals could not fire their shot
   the British bayonets would murder them.

There were supplies and powder they had stored
   at Warwick Furnace 20 miles away
however this would give the British force
   an open road to Philadelphia.

So Washington selected a detachment
   with General Wayne to hold the British back
in operations of delaying tactics
   to cause disruptions with a sneak attack.

As Washington directed a fast march
   to reach the stores of powder magazines
there was a fact he could not disregard
   that the whole cause was then in jeopardy.

He had to warn the Patriots in town
   that they must urgently evacuate
although the message would indeed announce
   a full admission that he had been beat.

George Washington knew this was more than him
   and he was willing to accept the loss
of life and reputation to defend
   the People's liberty and righteous cause.

So on the 19th Hamilton was sent
   to Philadelphia to give alert
of British forces launching an offense
   as their advancement could not be deterred.

The Congress easily could reconvene
   in any town within the countryside
and local Patriots could safely leave
   and so the cause for freedom could survive.

After restocking soldiers with supplies
   the Continentals crossed the Schuylkill River
and set to march back on the other side
   to try to catch up with the British army.

They heard bad news of General Wayne's detachment.
    Some Tories gave away their whereabouts
and British found the Patriot encampment
    and drove the Continentals in a rout.

And Howe was then positioned on the road
    before the town of Philadelphia
and waited for the Patriots' approach
    for an engagement with George Washington.

Then Hamilton returned to Washington
    informing that the Congress had escaped
and residents of faithful Patriots
    were also able to evacuate.

He also had supplies they stored on boats
    removed to safety on the Delaware
securing the provisions, gear and clothes
    and other articles for their repair.

So Alexander Hamilton had done
    all that had been assigned upon the task
to illustrate why General Washington
    gave him commission in commanding staff.

George Washington then chose not to engage.
    He knew the British would be fortified.
His men would charge into a cannonade
    and march directly into Howe's design.

So Washington worked to regain their strength,
    consolidate the troops and realign.
The British entered Philadelphia
    but Patriots controlled the countryside.

Chapter 42

The Battle of Germantown
October 4, 1777

George Washington was closely watching Howe
    while Continental forces built in strength
with the militias from surrounding towns
    and the detachment of Wayne's regiment.

September 26 the British moved
    and Philadelphia was occupied
but their main force was set 5 miles above
    at Germantown for a defensive line.

The British were amassed but seemed relaxed
    so early in October plans were made
for Continental forces to attack
    and storm the town before the break of day.

The Army would conduct a nighttime march
    approaching with 4 columns rapidly
and with the sudden onset in the dark
    converge upon the town decisively.

The two detachments of militia soldiers
    would march upon the far left and the right
engaging the reserves near Schuylkill River
    and hold them from supporting the front line.

Then two strong columns would march separately
    and then combine in strength upon approach
with Sullivan advancing on Main Street
    while General Greene would march down Lime Kiln Road.

At dusk October 3 the men filed in
   and set off marching in their regiments
that formed divisions of the columns set
   to strike the picket posts at 2 AM.

As picket posts were driven from their guard
   the sentries would alert the main defense
but by the time the British called alarm
   the columns would be driving down on them.

After midnight the 4 groups were on track
   of making their engagements right on time
and then ensued a series of set backs
   that wrenched apart the tactical design.

Greene drove the pickets set on Lime Kiln Road
   but then a regiment of infantry
set up defense so the advance was slowed
   and forced the column to halt suddenly.

Greene handled the obstruction expertly
   and built a force around the held position
then after pounding with artillery
   he cleared the area with the division.

The column moved again with the road clear
   but these maneuvers took some precious time
and up ahead the gunfire they could hear
   was indicating they were far behind.

The other column led by Sullivan
   was moving forward on the town's Main Street
and General Wayne was leading the advance
   that also ran into light infantry.

But from the sneak attack Wayne's men endured
    while Continentals marched to Warwick Furnace,
his regiment refused to be deterred
    and they were driving with their passions burning.

Then as Wayne's regiment pressed the approach
    the British infantry began to scatter.
They fired a frantic volley down the road
    and quickly drew back trying to re-gather.

Wayne's regiment was firing by platoons
    — one fired a volley, the next moved ahead
— reloading, marching, firing in a loop
    in steady, heavy incremental steps.

The British ranks and files could not reform.
    When they attempted to reorganize
a new platoon of musket fire would roar
    and send a volley tearing up their lines.

With Wayne's advance, one British regiment
    ran in a mansion known as the Chew House
in hopes to find some cover for defense
    while Patriots were driving through the town.

Divisions that were following Wayne's men
    were caught off guard by sudden musket fire
from the large house the British gathered in
    and had to stop the movement of the line.

They tried the cannons which had no effect,
    the field piece shot could not break the stone walls
and British muskets at each window ledge
    were striking soldiers at a heavy toll.

Then General Stirling led a noble charge
    to storm inside the fortress of a house
but they could not bust through the iron door
    while the grenades and shot were pouring down.

Wayne's regiment was running like a clock
    and chasing British forces with a drive
but Wayne became concerned they'd be cut off
    when he heard cannons firing from behind.

Then as Greene's column finally arrived
    a thick and heavy fog had billowed down
and General Stephen came up from behind
    where General Wayne was moving through the town.

Then General Stephens, who proved to be drunk,
    ordered his soldiers to commence to fire
and in the fog and smoke without a look
    shot straight into Wayne's regimental lines.

Then what was leading to a victory
    began to teeter as it fell apart
and British then reformed the infantry
    and quickly organized a counter charge.

Both sides of the militia weren't engaged
    so the reserves marched up to reinforce
and the momentum turned the British way
    as suddenly the battle changed in course.

Then as the columns began falling back
    George Washington sent orders for retreat
and the rear guard was blocking the attack
    to let the Army pull out orderly.

Chapter 43

Mud Island
October 1777

When General Washington had been informed
    that General Stephens was intoxicated
then Stephens promptly was placed on report
    and cashiered from the corps without probation.

With the turn of events at Germantown
    George Washington then changed his strategy
— with the initiative lost on the ground
    the British would entrench defensively.

Essentially the British were then trapped
    if Continentals blocked the British fleet.
The circumstance required that they adapt
    and Washington then set upon a siege.

They cleared the livestock 30 miles around
    and posted to deter the foraging
and held the Delaware outside of town
    to stop the fleet from bringing in relief.

They had two forts to guard the waterway.
    Fort Mercer stood upon New Jersey's shore
across the Delaware on the Red Banks
    and held 400 soldiers and their stores.

The other was Fort Mifflin on Mud Island,
    a mud flat settled downstream from a dike
and anchored with a palisade and cannons
    that barely crested water at high tide.

The soldiers labored hard with an endeavor,
    constructing a submerged *cheval-de-frise*
to block the fleet from sailing up the river
    and used bateaux to haul out every piece.

The British had about 300 ships
    they anchored at the Delaware's debouch
and Patriots had to build a defense
    to keep supplies from British shipping out.

And the artillery of the two forts
    could cover the obstruction in the stream
to block the ships from coming into port
    for the effectiveness to hold the siege.

So British began rolling cannons out
    to begin building several batteries
along the Delaware outside of town
    so that Fort Mifflin was in easy reach.

Then this required the soldiers on Mud Island
    to build more barricades to shield the fort
where all the strength was pointing down the river
    and unprepared for threats from their own shore.

Then General Howe pulled back from Germantown,
    retracting his perimeter defense
so he could send more men and cannons down
    to pulverize Fort Mifflin's battlements.

On Province Island within cannon range
    the British built up heavy armaments
and then bombarded throughout everyday
    for target practice on the Patriots.

The barracks and the blockhouses were shot
 so they were pummeled into splintered bits.
No one could safely rest upon a cot.
 They had to sleep inside a muddy ditch.

And then at night they labored in the dark,
 repairing damage from the cannonades
and after they refit the shattered parts
 they were destroyed again on the next day.

And mortar fire dropped bombs upon their heads
 and cannonballs were pounding on their works
and mud was smeared like butter on hard bread
 yet still the Continentals held the fort.

And vigilantly soldiers held their posts
 and manned the heavy guns that aimed downstream
to block the passage of the British boats
 while stationed on Mud Island through the siege.

Chapter 44

Fort Mercer
October 21-23, 1777

October 21 the British moved
    2000 Hessians to the Jersey shore
and organized formations of the troops
    to overwhelm Fort Mercer in a storm.

Then on the next day with the rising tide
    some British warships slowly moved upstream
and Hessian soldiers formed in battle lines
    late afternoon and close to evening.

The British planned to press upon the fort,
    coordinating effort on two sides
with Hessian forces pressing from the north
    supported by the heavy gunship fire.

The British ship *Augusta* lead the group
    with 64 long cannons in her hold
and was accompanied with smaller sloops
    that rode together up the tidal flow.

The ships maneuvered to negotiate
    the sunken lines of the *cheval-de-frise*
that served as an effective barricade
    to block approaches of the British fleet.

The Hessian leader ordered an advance
    since hours of afternoon were ebbing late
and marched for an assault with confidence
    before the naval guns came into range.

Fort Mercer had expansive outer works
    where riflemen could carefully take aim
and pinpoint Hessian soldiers in their march
    at lengths beyond the normal musket range.

Fort Mercer did not have the garrison
    with numbers to hold outer battlements.
The works however covered riflemen
    who riddled Hessian soldiers' confidence.

Then as the Hessian ranks were marching close
    the riflemen withdrew into the fort
and on the walls the sharp battalion rose
    after securing the fort's heavy doors.

Then on the river the small group of ships
    had tried to move by the *cheval-de-frise*
while fighting with the different elements
    of winds, stiff currents and the tides of sea.

3 times the Hessians tried to storm the fort.
    3 times the Hessian forces were repelled
with Continental cannons' loud reports
    of canister and the exploding shells.

And with the booming sounds of battle nigh
    the British ships tried for an urgent push
and the first ship passed an obstruction's line
    but could not move far up the river's rush.

By then the brilliance of the sun had set
    with the beginning of the turning tide
and the *Augusta* turned to ride the ebb
    back out to sea through cover of the night.

But in the early light of the next day
    the British ship *Augusta* did not move
and from the night was stuck in cannon range
    so the Mud Island heavy guns let loose.

They punched the hull with holes with red hot shot
    that they had heated in the well stoked fires
and soon some fires upon the boat had caught
    as smoke was rising through the rigging lines.

Another British boat came up to help
    but then the flames were rising from the deck
and sailors were abandoning the ship
    as fires on board began to leap and spread.

Soon masts and sails were totally in flames,
    then toppled as the fire consumed the boat
and touched the magazines to detonate
    and aftershock rose in a cloud of smoke.

With that, the ship had been completely cleared
    as flaming fragments flew into the air
and then the other had no better fare
    as it seemed to be stuck and had caught fire.

The second ship was then abandoned too
    and raging flames were burning for an hour
before the magazines of powder blew
    that sent a shock with the explosive power.

And both the forts were livened with loud cheers
    after the 2nd British ship had blown
and of the fleet that had been harbored near
    they only had 300 more to go.

The Hessian forces had withdrawn that day
  with heavy casualties from their assault
and the whole British fleet was held at bay
  by the 400 men who held the fort.

Chapter 45

Assignment and Reliance
October – November 1777

George Washington was closely watching Howe
  adjusting the positions of his troops
to see if any weakness could be found
  where Continental soldiers could break through.

Howe had retracted his defensive line
  to press upon the Continental forts
and as the troops were moved and realigned
  a gap could open to expose his corps.

But after the attack on Germantown
  the British force was moving cautiously
to cover every inch of the held ground
  so no gaps were left open carelessly.

George Washington had wanted to attack
  if he could find an advantageous place
but had to hold most of the Army back
  ensuring both the river forts were safe.

So both the armies moved in increments
  to carefully secure positions staked,
neither had numbers to launch an offense
  and hoped the other would make a mistake.

Then Washington heard good news from the north
  where General Gates had captured Burgoyne's army
and Continental cannons sent reports
  with *feu-de-joies* resounding through the country.

George Washington sent notice up to Gates
   commending his achievement and success
and Hamilton rode to communicate
   the message with esteem and great respect.

With the north Army's grand accomplishment
   they could return the men that were dispatched
so Washington could then regain the strength
   to threaten General Howe with an attack.

If Washington could press from the north side
   Howe would be forced to hold the Army back
and as the British reinforced the line
   the threats upon the forts would have to lapse.

The forts were in the critical position
   to block communications with the fleet
to stop the ammunition and provisions
   from reaching British forces in the siege.

George Washington gave Hamilton instructions
   to not impose on Gates if he had plans
but if he was not in a campaign's juncture
   to send down every serviceable man.

Soon Colonel Hamilton reached Putnam's camp
   positioned over the Manhattan isle
so regiments would march to Washington
   to keep Howe cut off through the winter time.

Putnam confirmed and said he would comply
   and then provided some key information
— the British at the New York harbor side
   appeared to be embarking reinforcements.

He did not know if they were sailing south,
    although it was a probability
and many saw the shipping heading out
    with several thousand British infantry.

Then Hamilton rode up to Albany
    to meet with Gates who camped with 4 brigades
and told the General of the urgency
    for troops to march to Philadelphia.

But General Gates would not let his men go
    yet did not have any impending plans
and Hamilton explained how General Howe
    was cornered with 12,000 of his men.

Then Hamilton said British reinforcements
    were seen embarking from the New York docks
but Gates thought they had planned attacking him
    as he secured an ammunition dump.

But the transports had sailed out from the bay,
    they were not heading up the Hudson River
as Alexander Hamilton explained
    from recent information he was given.

It was unlikely British would attack
    the distant magazines of ammunition
when their main army was pinned down and trapped
    without communications or provisions.

Yet Gates was the superior in rank
    so Hamilton requested for an order
and after an unwarranted delay
    Gates sent some troops of Continental soldiers.

When Hamilton returned to Putnam's camp
   the regiments he promised had not moved
although there was a critical demand
   for the assistance of the transferred troops.

The soldiers said their pay was in arrears,
   they had no wages for at least 6 months
and as it was the ending of the year
   they planned to build their winter quarters' huts.

So Hamilton met with the Governor
   of New York to secure a rightful loan
and with the soldiers paid, ordered a tour
   to try outmarching British transport boats.

Then Hamilton was leading regiments
   with Stars and Stripes and fifes and cadenced drums.
He did not simply have the message sent.
   He made for certain that the task was done.

Chapter 46

The End of the Year of the Hangman
November – December 1777

While Hamilton had travelled to New York
    recovering detachments of the men
George Washington worked to retain the forts
    while holding the defense of the mainland.

The Army personnel was stretched out thin
    with aims to keep the British force contained
but then Fort Mercer needed a defense
    in case another ground assault was made.

So Washington had General Varnum sent
    to guard the two key forts with his brigade
and hoped for the arrival of more men
    so they could bolster strength in the blockade.

Then on November 10 there were reports
    of heavy cannon fire below the town
with the bombardment of Mud Island's fort
    that had commenced before the break of dawn.

The British had lined up 6 batteries
    200 yards from the Mud Island post.
Each had 6 pieces of artillery
    and fired the guns as fast as they could load.

Fort Mifflin on Mud Island had endured
    a regular bombardment for a month
but unexpectedly that morning turned
    with cannonades that seemed more vigorous.

And solid shot was bouncing all around
   and smashing in the sides of palisades
as mortar bombs continued dropping down
   and bursting everywhere throughout the day.

And the brave Patriots sent their replies
   with well served guns that fired the shot right back
except one cannon quiet at the side
   that was the largest cannon that they had.

They did not have the 32 pound shot
   that fit the gun's specific caliber
until a soldier eagerly had brought
   a cannonball he found on the far shore.

It seemed the British had the same gun gauge
   and officers sent soldiers on the hunt
and every ball returned with the same make
   would be rewarded with a gill of rum.

The soldiers who were not held in the front
   began to scour Mud Island's lea side shore
but soon realized the British big bore gun
   was raking the parade ground of the fort.

So then the soldiers lined up on the flat
   and taunted British from the open lot
and drew the fire so they could send it back
   while chasing balls till they rolled to a stop.

All through the day the soldiers stood and waved
   and waited for the next incoming shot
then dodged and scrambled on the wide parade
   and later savored rum the prize had bought.

The only time the cannonade slowed down
    was after sunset and the daylight's end
and then the next day at the break of dawn
    the tireless cannonade began again.

This ceaseless pounding lasted 5 long days
    but then there was a change on the 15th
and twilight time the soldiers were awake
    as 8 ships came up from the British fleet.

The barricades they planted in the river
    had changed the current of the Delaware
and cleared the draft of ships up to Mud Island
    that rode upon the flood tide unawares.

6 of the ships had 64 guns each
    and one had 6, another 24
and set 100 yards off of the beach
    and began opening their porthole doors.

The few fort guns that still remained in service
    began to open fire upon the ships
but soon the place was hotter than a furnace
    as all the British guns began to rip.

The 8 gunships with the 6 batteries
    erupted with a roaring cannonade
with the resolved intent, undoubtedly,
    to blow the fort and island both away.

The cannon fire kept up incessantly.
    The shot was pounding every inch of ground.
The air was filled with searing metal screams
    that knocked Fort Mifflin's cannons off the mounts.

The blockhouses and barracks were in flames
  as bombs exploded everywhere around
and stone was pulverized in palisades
  with sections of the walls collapsing down.

The sailors climbed the rigging of the masts
  and fired at any Patriot they saw
and even hand grenades were being casts
  the ships were so close to Fort Mifflin's walls.

This cataclysm kept up the whole day
  — guns firing faster than a rolling drum,
yet still the Stars and Stripes were on display
  and the fort's Patriots did not give up.

By night the scene was utter devastation.
  The fort's last cannons were knocked off there mounts
and soldiers lined up for evacuation
  escaping cross the river on bateaux.

The British reinforcements had arrived
  and then Cornwallis organized his troops
across the river on the Jersey side
  and movement on Fort Mercer had ensued.

Since all the men Cornwallis organized
  arrived on transports sailing from New York
he did not weaken Howe's defensive line
  by drawing men from Howe's positioned corps.

This kept George Washington on the defensive
  and limited support he could detach
and without reinforcements of more men
  Fort Mercer's soldiers had to be called back.

Directly after the siege had collapsed
   the men recovered from Gates had arrived
but then the opportunity had passed
   and ships refreshed the British with supplies.

Then snow was drifting through the icy winds
   and General Washington marched with his corps.
As one year ends another will begin
   with winter quarters held at Valley Forge.

1778

Chapter 47

Valley Forge
Winter 1778

At Valley Forge the men constructed huts
    for shelter from the winter elements
and gaps between the slats were stuffed with mud
    in hopes to block the snow and sleet and wind.

Inside the huts the men tried to keep warm
    but tiny fires would choke the air with smoke
yet stepping out while gasping for fresh air,
    they'd frieze to death in torn and tattered clothes.

There were some men with nothing but a shirt,
    3000 men did not have shoes or boots
and without blankets most slept on the dirt
    while shivering from drafts and dripping roofs.

The soldiers suffered through the agony
    where marches in the snow were tracked with blood
from bootless feet of many infantry
    who wrapped their feet with rags the best they could.

Then the torment of the infernal itch
    inflicted every Continental man
as lice gnawed mercilessly on the skin
    while trapped all winter in the lousy camp.

They went to winter quarters without beef.
    Of flour barrels – they had 25.
All the 10,000 soldiers had to eat
    were wafer cakes they roasted by the fires.

Some men were cutting up each cartridge box
   and chewing on the little shreds of leather
or boiling it to try to make a broth
   for anything to ease the hollowed hunger.

And many of the men had cherished homes
   with wives and children and supplies of stores
yet still endured the misery and cold
   for duty with the Continental corps.

And General Washington was at the camp
   and said that through their courage, strength and faith
the men were proving their own worthiness
   for independence they fought to obtain.

The General shared the spirit with the men
   for civil liberty they fought to win
but as the loyal men had followed him,
   in the command he must take care of them.

A soldier lives a vigorous lifestyle
   — no one develops strength through leisure ease,
but the conditions of the men were dire
   from no neglect of their abilities.

Committees of the Congress visited
   to see the commissaries carelessness
and then the quartermaster had not been
   providing clothes he had been promising.

George Washington maintained the protocol
   fulfilling duties, just as did his men,
but all the People were responsible
   for earning the new nation's benefits.

They had embarked upon a single cause
    with challenges demanding unity,
each person of the nation plays a role
    to gain and then maintain their liberty.

To soldiers, Washington exemplified
    the powerful resolve of character
and with his constant presence emphasized
    the dignity and honor that they earned.

The General wrote to the state Governors
    to make the explanations clear and plain
for the whole country to support the corps
    that is defending the United States.

Then answering George Washington's request
    the Congress had replaced the quartermaster,
appointing someone with more willingness
    to help improve conditions for the soldiers.

They could not fight on principles alone.
    They needed practical necessities.
The soldiers fought for all the People's homes
    yet everyone must work for victory.

And General Washington fulfilled his role
    through difficulties and abject heartbreak
so that the bell of liberty may toll,
    inaugurating the United States.

Chapter 48

The Conway Cabal
January – April 1778

Throughout the struggles of the winter time
   with scant supplies and brutal, winter weather
some sinister ideas rose in the minds
   of a few malcontents against their leader.

They looked upon the course of the campaign
   and concentrated on deficiencies,
convinced that if they all had their own way
   the battles would have turned out differently.

Extracting pieces of particulars
   from the scenarios of past events
they tore what had transpired in tiny parts
   to fabricate ideal alternatives.

Then through perspectives of a narrow view
   they were convinced that the entirety
of what they felt for certain that they knew
   encompassed every possibility.

A number of the officers took note
   and spoke in confidence with Washington
of mutinous ambitions on the boat
   and how designs of plots were being drawn.

A new appointment for Inspector General
   — a gentleman by name of Thomas Conway,
had wrote some messages sent confidential
   to slander the Commander and the Council.

He had complained of the incompetence
    in matters that he did not understand
and glancing over singular events
    felt that he had conceived a failsafe plan.

He felt that General Gates should be in charge
    and General Washington should be removed.
The singular defeat of Burgoyne's march
    should be admitted as conclusive proof.

George Washington knew the significance
    of plans to sever the United States,
that's why he sent his finest regiments
    to bolster the position held by Gates.

George Washington acknowledged General Gates
    and did not claim the credit for the win.
His job required that he administrate.
    The battle had been won by all the men.

All the decisions Washington had made
    accounted for the national defense.
He was not simply helping General Gates.
    He was defending national interests.

Conway was making a naive mistake
    by passing judgement on what he believed
when management of the United States
    involved bewildering complexities.

George Washington responded candidly
    and notified Conway of what he learned.
He was a man of stern integrity
    and had no time to quibble the absurd.

George Washington apprised the Congressmen
    so all the delegates had been informed,
addressing questions with his selflessness
    which was the nature of his character.

And Washington suggested a review
    to measure his performance in command
and an evaluation could conclude
    the General's honesty and competence.

Around that time some papers went in print
    where an anonymous press made the claim
that they found letters Washington had sent
    against the cause of the United States.

The letters proved to be a forgery
    but incidentally made the admission
— the greatest worry of the enemy
    was General Washington's command commission.

By April General Conway had resigned,
    the cabal was exposed and flit away
and Washington stayed focused the whole time,
    preparing the men for the next campaign.

Chapter 49

Feu-de-Joie
May 6, 1778

The 6th of May the soldiers were surprised
  with special orders forming for assembly
and soldiers fell into their ranks and files
  to hear the chaplains speak to each battalion.

The grounds of camp were trampled, muddy paths
  where soldiers had been treading everyday
and miseries of winter storms had passed
  as spring awakened with the warmth of May.

Nathanael Greene was made the quartermaster
  and soldiers finally received supplies.
Of course the means remained austere and meager
  but they at least had food to stay alive.

And Friedrich Steuben organized new drills
  that soldiers practiced regimentally
with daily exercises on the field
  to operate with uniformity.

As icy weather passed, they gathered strength
  arising with the hope of new prospects.
The winter pushed them back unto the brink
  and as they held they could then move ahead.

There were no chapels with neat pews in rows,
  the soldiers were assembled in their ranks
and stood attentively as chaplains spoke
  to lead the soldiers in thanksgiving grace.

The soldiers were surprised that services
    were held on Wednesday that time of the year
and why battalions solemnly addressed
    began erupting in exalted cheers.

In time each Army chaplain had declared
    that France had recognized the independence
of the United States of America
    and the two nations had formed an alliance.

With soldiers given the triumphant word
    so the good news was reverently taught
George Washington made sure the soldiers heard
    this was accredited a gift of God.

When chapel services came to an end
    the General Orders for the day were made.
A signal cannon made report again
    and soldiers were reformed into their ranks.

The officers inspected arms and dress
    while adjuncts were recording careful notes
so staff could then compile a thorough list
    of needed gear and articles of clothes.

After inspection there was a report
    — a single cannon signaling the troops
to march into their battle lines and form
    in two broad columns for parade review.

And the two columns marched with cadenced steps
    that had been tuned and polished with their drill
and halted with the sharp alignment set
    with uniformity across the field.

Then 13 cannons sounded with a roar
  for the United States in perfect time
and signaled the salute of the whole corps
  in executing a tight rolling fire.

Beginning from the right each regiment
  was ordered by their officers to fire
and rolled out to the left in sequencing
  of perfect timing passing down the line.

And as each regiment had sounded off
  the second line was given its own turn
and from the left to right the musket shot
  moved through the regiments in a return.

Each regiment reported orderly
  like skillful steps of an artistic dance
and then the corps resounded volubly
  as soldiers bellowed a huzzah for France.

Then they repeated this two times again
  in marshalled repetition without breaks
— again for all their European friends
  and then once more for the United States.

Then Washington had soldiers reconnoiter
  for movements near by Philadelphia
as he anticipated British orders
  to quit their post in Pennsylvania.

George Washington heard General Howe transferred
  as he requested to return to England
and then both Congress and the General learned
  that Howe's command had gone to General Clinton.

The British had declared a war on France
    who also had a massive naval fleet.
The British had to strengthen their defense
    as now they had a threat upon the sea.

The ships were leaving down the Delaware
    and packed with Tories anxious to depart
and without any shipping space to spare
    the British soldiers had no choice but march.

As British ships were sailing from the port,
    then Clinton was seen organizing ranks
as he would have to hurry to New York
    so British forces could consolidate.

So Washington was waiting patiently
    for British to march out with their full force.
With their divisions filing in retreat
    they'd struggle for their battle lines to form.

The British would be stretched out on the road
    and Washington could take them piece by piece
and hopefully they'd never reach New York
    to join their garrison of infantry.

George Washington kept the whole corps prepared
    and set for a deployment rapidly
then Patriots formed up with arms and gear
    as British began marching June 18.

Chapter 50

Balancing Judgement
June 1778

As British forces crossed the Delaware
   George Washington advanced to intercept
and Patriots marched with their arms and gear
   in rank and file that drummed in cadenced steps.

The miseries of wintertime had passed
   with shivered cold and aches for lack of food.
The sense of purpose was renewed at last
   — the Continental corps was on the move.

At Valley Forge the soldiers were annealed
   with heavy hammer blows of elements
and polished into shiny steel through drills
   with edges keen to get to business.

Maxwell's brigade was sent for skirmishing
   to harry British movements with delays
so Washington could gain positioning
   upon the country roadways and terrain.

The Continentals crossed into New Jersey
   upstream the Delaware by 30 miles
to transport heavy cannons on a ferry
   along a northward route to give more time.

Then on the 24th they held a Council
   of War with the commanders of the Army
as they were in position to encounter
   the British in retreat to New York harbor.

Amongst the Generals joining Washington,
    Charles Lee had been restored into the ranks
after a swap of captured officers
    had been negotiated and arranged.

Although Lee had his eccentricities
    George Washington respected his advice
but was surprised when Lee had disagreed
    about engaging British for a fight.

Lee felt that the alliance made with France
    would give them all the troops that they would need.
It was not necessary to advance.
    The British could rejoin their naval fleet.

Charles Lee was an old friend of Washington
    and he made a good point to back his case
that since the British march was moving slow
    they must have set a trap or ambuscade.

George Washington was open for advice
    and although stern, he was not obstinate.
His reason balanced judgement at all times
    while neither timid nor impetuous.

But in this case the General disagreed.
    In their retreat, the British were exposed
and when the British joined back with their fleet
    it would be hard for them to be deposed.

They could not wait for France to send them help.
    They had to seize the opportunity.
The British force was then assailable
    and they could gain a major victory.

George Washington planned a detail attack
  so British could not line up their full force
and 1400 soldiers were detached
  along with General Scott to reinforce.

The soldiers led by Scott would join Maxwell
  to reconnoiter movement and position
and skirmish with the British in details
  along the road with menacing resistance.

Then on the 25th there was a message
  that British soldiers were approaching Monmouth
and with the march's slow and lengthy progress
  they were expected to file past the courthouse.

George Washington dispatched 2000 men
  to reinforce the troops already sent
along with the Marquis de Lafayette
  and issued orders that he take command.

George Washington instructed Lafayette
  not to attack till British left the town.
They did not want the British force to set
  so they become entrenched to hold the ground.

Then on the 27th General Lee
  met privately with General Washington,
protesting the young Frenchman in the lead.
  As senior, Lee felt he should have command.

So Washington agreed to send Charles Lee
  with an additional 2000 men
to take command as the detachment's lead
  to form and order them for an offense.

Then General Washington was very clear
   how Lee's detachment needed to engage
— they were the tip of the whole Army's spear
   but the whole Army must coordinate.

Lee needed to wait till the British marched
   and then engage them while they're on the road
with an attack upon their troops' rear guard
   so the detachment of their corps would hold.

The General did not want the British ranks
   to have a chance to form in battle lines
then in their marching files along the way
   the British could be struck with a surprise.

Then Washington would bring the Army up
   and with the full corps they would overwhelm
the whole detachment of the British troops
   and then completely sweep the battlefield.

Then if the forward British troops turned back
   the Army would be set for a defense
and in position to block the attack
   and knock down each brigade as they marched in.

When Lee arrived near where the British camped
   they changed the disposition of their march
and moved the strongest British regiments
   into position at their troops' rear guard.

Then on the 27th at sunset
   Lee had the regiments set into place
in preparation for the planned offense
   when British broke their camp and were away.

Chapter 51

Monmouth: Catastrophe
June 28, 1778 (morning)

The 28th of June before daylight
   Colonel John Lauren notified Charles Lee
the British soldiers formed in marching lines
    and the rear guard was packed and on their feet.

The soldiers hopped from their night's bivouacs.
   They were prepared. They slept upon their arms.
The British lines were set a few miles back
    and Continentals formed in ranks to march.

Out front was General Varnum's strong brigade
   and General Lee was riding close behind
as soldiers marched a strident eager pace
    — they suffered through the winter for this fight.

At the far left was General Dickinson
   who led the Jersey men in the militia
and at the right was Colonel Morgan's men
    with rifle marksmen hailing from Virginia.

And there was some contest for which would reach
   the open field of the engagement first
in rivalries of camaraderie
    that strengthened the whole body of the corps.

But then the troops with Varnum fell behind
   as they were forced to file across a bridge
and the broad column squeezed into a line
    while Dickinson and Morgan edged ahead.

After they crossed the soldiers were reformed
    and once again advanced in unison
with the entire coordinated force
    that aimed momentously upon the front.

But then as Varnum's men were underway,
    after they managed the impediment,
a countermarch by General Lee was made
    to turn them back across the bridge again.

Then every regiment came to a halt
    and once again they narrowed to a file
as Varnum had reorganized them all
    to form again upon the other side.

When Varnum asked Charles Lee what had been wrong
    Lee said he saw a movement in the woods
and was concerned that they would be cut off
    which Varnum privately thought was absurd.

Then General Lee said that the coast was clear
    and Varnum should continue in advance,
there seemed to be nothing that they should fear
    and filed across the bridge once more again.

When Varnum's men reformed for the 3rd time
    and finally resumed to move ahead
they were more than a mile from the front line
    and they could hear the skirmishing begin.

By 8 AM in the bright morning light
    both Dickinson and Morgan were engaged
and British ranks began to organize
    but General Lee and the main force was late.

The Patriots had a small cavalry
  and they were on the field in their full force
but without Continental infantry
  there was no Army that they could support.

Then from the road that led to Middletown
  the heavy British cavalry arrived
and quickly formed upon the open ground
  far larger than the Continental's size.

So the light cavalry of Patriots
  withdrew from their position on the field
as the dragoons began to make a charge
  and quickly crested over a back hill.

Then cavalry was then relieved to see
  from the perspective of the hill above
the Continentals marching rapidly
  as Varnum's infantry was coming up.

The officers drew out the firing lines
  and as the British cavalry pursued
the Continentals launched a volley fire
  as galloping dragoons came into view.

The British quickly turned for a retreat
  as horses without riders shirked away
and then two pieces of artillery
  set on the hilltop and began to play.

Then Varnum sent some groups of infantry
  to post before the cannons for support
but this was countermanded by Charles Lee
  who sent them on an oblique circuit tour.

This left the cannons open and exposed
    and baffled Varnum with perplexity
but Lee said that he sent them to the road
    to block the British infantry's retreat.

But Lee's response did not make any sense.
    Why would he send the troops off to the back
to capture the retreating British men?
    They hadn't even formed for an attack!

Then Lee began to order on the field
    the different regiments of the brigade.
Each order that he gave he'd then repeal
    while pointlessly adjusting every place.

Three regiments that were set on the right
    were ordered forward to make an advance
and as they began marching in a line
    he quickly sent his staff to countermand.

Then Lee gave orders for them to retire
    and march to Monmouth where they would reform
then changed again and had them turn their line
    to march into the woods and send reports.

While Dickinson and Morgan pressed the flanks
    with companies of rifled skirmishers
the British began ordering their ranks
    and centered their main strength to make a charge.

So General Lee then ordered a retreat
    but did not notify some officers
and half the messages were not received
    and no one could believe what they had heard.

One half the force upon the field of ranks
    was waiting for the signal to attack
then stood confused as other regiments
    had turned around and began marching back.

Then as the British began to advance
    the other regiments had to withdraw
and no one in the troops could understand
    how they had lost a fight they never fought.

The soldiers who were first in the retreat
    saw General Washington arrive in haste,
he had been galloping upon his steed
    and stopped at the first soldier on the way.

He asked the man why they were in retreat.
    The soldier simply said he did not know.
They never had engaged the enemy.
    He did not even fire his musket load.

Then Washington told all the men to hold,
    instructing officers into position
and then continued sprinting up the road
    to see the soldiers' overall condition.

George Washington was able to spot Lee
    and Lee said the attack was ill advised.
Both he and the War Council disagreed
    with both the strategy and the design.

George Washington turned red throughout his face
    but still maintained himself with steadfast will
— a mountain that would neither budge nor break,
    then sternly said that Lee must leave the field.

Chapter 52

Monmouth: Victory
June 28, 1778 (afternoon)

George Washington rode to a prominence
    for an assessment of the battle scene
and soldiers in the corps of the advance
    were taking heat in a confused retreat.

It seemed that Lee had left half of the men
    with the formation of the corps undone
and as the British guns were bombing them
    they did not know if they should fight or run.

Then officers of British batteries
    saw Washington upon his horse exposed
and ordered to direct artillery
    to knock the leader off the horse he rode.

And as the British guns were finding range
    the General viewed the men with his field glass
and paid no heed to cannons turned his way
    and counted British in their lines' attack.

The solid shot was screeching by the hill
    and cannon balls were tearing through the turf
but Washington was focused on the field
    and calmed his neighing horse that was disturbed.

George Washington saw ranks of grenadiers
    with the light infantry and the chasseurs
supported by the heavy cavalry
    as General Clinton sent his strongest troops.

The cannonballs were pounding all around
    as Washington could see the field was clear
but then the British line was coming down
    and he had to make sure they were prepared.

So Washington rode down amongst the men
    and ordered two brigades into position
behind a hedgerow and a country fence
    to hold the British with a strong resistance.

George Washington spoke with the officers
    to emphasize the dire necessity
of holding tight and adamantly firm
    till the main Army comes for their relief.

The Continentals marched in double time
    and would arrive with the full Army's force
then organize to set their battle lines
    into position to provide support.

So General Varnum's men were set in place
    with cannons lined up on the hill behind
and officers checked details as they paced
    awaiting for the British to arrive.

Then in the distance beyond rifle range
    the British lined up as their numbers built
and formed an order of outstretching ranks
    to press the setting of the battlefield.

It is a slow, methodic exercise
    with care both volatile and delicate
like setting powder kegs to build a spire
    before the detonating fuse is lit.

And Varnum's officers were shouting out
    that every soldier must wait for commands
and make sure that their charges were tamped down
    and all together they would make a stand.

They had to hold their fire until close range
    — till they could count the buttons on the coats,
and steady their composure as they wait
    to manage strength with disciplined control.

No one could fire until he heard the order
    and everyone must aim before he shot.
Each man relied upon his fellow soldier
    and all together they were solid rock.

Then British regiments began to march
    and many soldiers called out "Here they come!"
and the artillery prepared each charge
    to carefully position the big guns.

They loaded solid shot for the approach
    to try to thin the British ranks from far
and then as the advance was marching close
    they'd spray the field with grape and canisters.

Then suddenly they heard off to the side
    a thundering of countless pounding hooves
as British cavalry ran on the right
    to flank the Patriots with the dragoons.

The cannons did not have time to adjust.
    They were not loaded with the grape they'd need
but Colonel Olney had two regiments
    that stood before the charging cavalry.

The cavalry was tearing cross the field,
    the sharpened saber blades were raised and gleaming
and in the summer heat, the flashing steel
    was drawn to cut the Patriots to pieces.

And Colonel Olney yelled out for his men
    to reassure their hold and steady them
and hoof beats loudened and were thundering
    like an immense tornado rushing in.

One force was plunging forward at full speed.
    The other was positioned to hold fast.
Dragoons were roaring forward on their steeds
    and keening on the edge where they would clash.

Then Colonel Olney ordered them to aim
    and muzzles leveled at the monstrous sight
approaching less than 50 yards away
    then Olney hollered for his men to fire.

A fiery volley leapt with muzzle flames
    and the dragoons ran straight into a wall
and the ferocious storm of saber blades
    was dashed to pieces with the musket balls.

So the attempt to break the troops apart
    before the British infantry arrived
had failed before it had a chance to start
    thanks to the Colonel and his solid line.

By then the batteries were in full play
    as British grenadiers came into range
and lashed the British march with cannonades
    to try to hold the grenadiers at bay.

But stubbornly the British force advanced
    while moving forward in short increments
and built up strength nearby for an offense
    while setting batteries supporting them.

The grenadiers then concentrated force
    and launched into a furious foray
but General Varnum's soldiers slammed the door
    and scattered grenadiers in disarray.

But British were continuing to build
    and although Varnum had a strong position,
they would be challenged to secure the field
    as British were amassing a division.

Then British batteries began to fire
    and solid shot was thick in the barrage
and Varnum yelled for them to hold the line
    beneath the flying shrapnel of the bombs.

The light field battery of Varnum's corps
    was struggling to match the British guns
and the large British force began to form
    and they would soon be ready to come up.

And General Varnum bolstered up his men
    preparing them to fight off the attack.
They would not back away a single inch.
    Whatever Britain gave, they'd give more back.

Then suddenly George Washington rode up
    and General Varnum snapped a sharp salute
and then saw Stirling rolling in more guns
    with lines of soldiers marching into view.

Then to the right Greene set up batteries
    as his division also had arrived
and then the leverage of artillery
    set firmly on the Continental's side.

Then with the Continentals in position
    George Washington alerted the command
that they were ready for a general movement
    to execute the Patriots' advance.

That afternoon the fighting was intense
    as Washington commanded the attack
and orchestrated movements of the men
    and step by step they pushed the British back.

And in this epic struggle of mankind
    there were a number of brave women too
and many were close to the battle lines
    and risked their lives for independence too.

And in this battle Mary Ludwig Hays
    was helping Continental batteries
and fearlessly was working in the fray
    and has been noted throughout history.

Then British soldiers were forced to retreat.
    The Continental Army held the field.
Then General Washington arrested Lee
    and ordered a Court Martial to be held.

1779

Chapter 53

Colonel Clark's Frontier Expedition

George Clark was born in Charlottesville, Virginia
    and grew up at a local, country farm
then volunteered to join in the militia
    and was commissioned Colonel for the war.

Intrepidly exploring the frontier
    he mapped terrain through the Ohio Valley
and settled in the wilderness for years
    and built a farm in what would be Kentucky.

And far beyond the Appalachian range
    detached across the vast expansive land
the frontier settlements that had been made
    were pillaged and destroyed by ruthless bands.

George Roger Clark then travelled to Virginia
    and had a talk with state authorities
for the approval of an expedition
    after he had explained his strategy.

The British had control of some outposts
    set on important river passageways
and Clark was confident he could depose
    the British presence in the wild terrain.

The campaign he intended would be small.
    He wouldn't need more than 200 men.
There were a few supplies that they would haul
    and then could hunt for staple sustenance.

So people in Virginia had agreed
    to make assignments for some volunteers,
equipping the detachment modestly
    and sent them with George Clark to the frontier.

Then at Pittsburg they loaded in small boats
    to cruise the Allegheny and Ohio.
The waterways were the exclusive roads
    upon the journey for 1000 miles.

Then the campaign arrived at Fort Massac
    — with numbers of 180 men
and Colonel Clark led them along deer paths
    120 miles through wilderness.

They took the British outposts by surprise
    — Kaskaskia, Cahokia, Vincennes
and following Clark's tactical designs
    they captured every posted garrison.

Then Canada's Lieutenant Governor
    — a British man named Henry Hamilton,
received a message sent to Fort Detroit
    reporting battles Patriots had won.

So Hamilton detached 500 men
    and took command of the offensive force
and travelled on the Wabash to Vincennes
    to capture the strategically placed fort.

The Wabash River was a crucial line
    between the Mississippi and Great Lakes,
accessing some vast tracts of country side
    where British needed to communicate.

With the Americans set in Vincennes
   they had command of the whole watershed
— a massive portion of the continent
   with the Ohio Valley wilderness.

With the small numbers of George Clark's command
   Vincennes was held by only a few men
and they were driven out by Hamilton
   whose large detachment fortified defense.

George Roger Clark had stationed his main force
   at camp more than a hundred miles away
in a position near the Illinois
   and they were eager for a new campaign.

In early February Colonel Clark
   assembled a small group of infantry
who gathered baggage with their gear and arms,
   prepared to venture expeditiously.

Clark had a galley loaded with supplies
   that he would signal later for relief
but British would secure the waterside
   and Clark had planned a different strategy.

So Colonel Clark prepared his men to march
   to make their own path through the wilderness
and catch the British soldiers off their guard
   with an attack that they would not expect.

Chapter 54

Making a Way
February 5-18, 1779

The 5th of February they set out
   with Colonel Clark in charge of the command
— 170 men by his count
   to capture the Vincennes' garrison.

With trains of horses packing the supplies
   they set off in the rugged wilderness,
a chartless journey for 100 miles
   while hunting the wild game for sustenance.

As they were marching Clark sent companies
   to venture from the group to hunt for deer
then nightly gathered for the bounty's feast
   for all the soldiers to enjoy and share.

The march was tough while slogging through the mud
   and daily hunts provided a relief
from the conditions of the winter month
   with the contests of friendly rivalries.

Each company tried to outdo the others
   while bringing in the game of sporting hunts,
providing venison for all the soldiers
   while competition kept their spirits up.

They crossed a waterway on the 13th
   — a tributary of the Wabash River
and trudged 5 miles to find a place to sleep
   on a high point above the chilly water.

Then when they reached the Wabash River edge
  there was a high embankment for a camp
but looking onward gave a sense of dread
  as they saw the expanse of flooded swamp.

All day they slogged across the flooded plain
  in hope to find a dry place they could sleep
and often water was up to their waist
  and never lowered less than 2 feet deep.

They found a patch of high ground near the river,
  a half mile island on the endless moors
and some were casting doubt on the endeavor
  and Clark knew their position was then poor.

What Clark had felt he kept unto himself.
  The worrisome and doubtful had no worth.
The way to overcome the difficult
  is through good reasoning and earnest work.

So Clark made sure the soldiers were engaged
  to keep their heads above the murky doubt.
They needed to traverse the water way,
  so he had some men fashion a dugout.

They'd use the dugout to explore the swamp
  so they could find where their next camp would set,
and as they made their journey to Vincennes
  they'd clear this mess with their accomplishments.

Over the river men were laboring
  at the embankment where the group would cross
and notched some logs to build a scaffolding
  so the transported gear would not be lost.

Then on the dugout men went to explore
    for the next place the march could make a camp
and marked the trees with chipping hatchet scores
    to guide the way along the flooded path.

The 15th they had crossed the Wabash River
    and followed the tree marks to the high ground
and the accomplishment boosted their spirits
    as they felt no hardship could hold them down.

What they had viewed to be a daunting task
    was then a triumph of a major feat
and overcome, the challenges then passed
    to affirmation of capacity.

And Clark was pleased to hear the soldiers jest
    with affirmation of what they had done
while entertained with antics of one man
    who floated in the water on his drum.

Then on the 18th up before the sun
    the soldiers were reminded of their mission
when they had heard the British morning gun
    resounding through the forest from the distance.

The dugout was dispatched by Colonel Clark
    to notify the galley to come up
and then the Colonel had the soldiers start
    to build canoes in case the boat was stuck.

They could not wait for the boat to arrive
    and risk detection of their stealth approach.
Without the element of the surprise
    the garrison might not be overthrown.

The garrison had several hundred men
   who held the British fortified position
but this did not upset Clark's confidence
   that they would be successful in the mission.

His confidence was not complacency,
   as if the battle was already won.
He simply was determined to succeed
   because he knew the task had to be done.

Chapter 55

The Sugar Camp
February 21, 1779

The march's prospects on the 21st
    appeared to many cynics to be grim
and some discouraging concerns were heard
    that were influencing the weaker men.

They knew they were 3 miles from the next camp
    but the canoes returned with doubtful news
— the flooded sections were too deep to stand
    and they could not find any passage through.

Of course Clark found this unacceptable.
    There is no stopping ingenuity.
What some resign to be impossible
    is the sure sigh of opportunity.

So Colonel Clark went out to check himself
    and sounded water depths on a canoe
and places were as deep as to his neck
    but still he knew they were not destitute.

While focusing on what could not be done,
    the cynics could not see a passage through,
but thinking how the battle could be won
    Clark only focused on what they could do.

He took his time returning to the camp
    to contemplate their means and situation
so they could venture through their confidence
    while navigating by the complications.

If water was too deep for them to march,
   they'd ferry themselves on canoes to cross.
It'd take all day and well into the dark
   but his men's passage through would not be blocked.

Returning to the camp Clark saw the men
   all standing at the shore expectantly
to hear what Colonel Clark would say to them
   of the predicament's severity.

George Roger Clark was thinking quietly
   which caused some of the men to hesitate
and as the men were waiting anxiously
   the Colonel stumbled with a slight mistake —

instead of first addressing all the troops
   he whispered something to an officer
and many of the cynics misconstrued
   this as the proof of the impossible.

Most of the men refused to be disturbed
   and waited for what Colonel Clark would say.
But many of the cynics were unnerved
   and they began bewailing in dismay.

The soldiers did not know what Clark had said
   but some were so convinced with their beliefs,
frenetically they misinterpreted
   each shadow as substantial certainty.

Some were dramatic and hysterical
   while most the men were looking on perplexed
at why the cynics were out of control
   and always slipping in distressing fits.

Clark knew these problems could not be contained.
   The matter would not mend with help or force.
If he tried pulling at the frets and frays
   his efforts would just worsen what was torn.

Clark was surrounded by his officers
   and the large group of his Kentucky men,
then Clark said so those closest to him heard —
   to watch and do exactly what he did.

Clark stepped out so that everyone could see
   and those who were hysteric stopped to watch
as they were groping for some fixity,
   then Colonel Clark gave meaning to the pause.

The Colonel poured some powder in his hand
   then splashed a little water for a paste
and looking fiercely at the group of men
   began to smear the powder on his face.

Then Clark let out a bellowing war whoop
   then grabbed his bag and snatched up his flintlock
and walked directly in the flooded woods
   and no one there had doubt of his resolve.

All the Kentucky men shouted, "Huzzah!"
   then grabbed their guns and followed in a line.
They had no interest staying in the swamp.
   They'd only reach the high ground if they climbed.

Then as the former camp was filed away
   the group refusing earlier to go
had quietly decided to be brave
   — they were more scared of being left alone.

Although Clark walked directly in the swamp,
　　he knew by night they'd climb back on dry land.
He was not risking that his men might drown.
　　He sloshed into the water with a plan.

But Clark realized if he tried to explain
　　it would not matter what he had to say.
The cynics love to hear themselves complain.
　　To get this done Clark had to show a way.

They'd march the most they could to make best time
　　then ferry cross the places that were deep
but suddenly when water was waist high
　　a soldier felt a trail beneath his feet.

He felt the settled path of game and tread
　　and other men confirmed what he had found
as they could feel the route the trail way led
　　that seemed to travel on the higher ground.

So then the file turned on the flooded trail
　　and what some thought would be impossible
turned out to be a fairly easy day
　　as the expected problems had been solved.

Then after they had passed through a few miles
　　they walked up on 10 acres of dry land
and warmed and dried beside their kindled fires
　　while resting early at the Sugar Camp.

Chapter 56

A Mind–Set for Victory
February 22-23, 1779

That night at Sugar Camp there was a freeze
    and ice had formed around the water's edge
and as the men awakened from their sleep
    the British morning gun was heard ahead.

With the spare breakfast few men said a word,
    they were too weary to make conversation
and through the difficulties they endured
    some wondered if they'd reach their destination.

The officers and sergeants had them pack
    and gather baggage as they broke the camp
and they could hear the ice make shivered cracks
    as light was brightening the swampy land.

Then all the soldiers crowded up to Clark
    to hear the plans and orders of the day.
The Colonel clearly was prepared to start
    and a blunt explanation was then made:

"Men, we have trudged through swamps 100 miles
    and cross this plain and past those distant trees
is our sought object and our labor's prize
    and will soon end our arduous fatigue."

George Roger Clark confirmed what they had done
    and pointed to remind them of their goal
then broke the ice by marching with his gun
    out on the plain into the lively cold.

The ice was crushed beneath the Colonel's feet
   and as he marched into the open plain
the water stood no more than ankle deep
   and Clark made way and did not hesitate.

The men then hollered out a loud "Huzzah!"
   and filed behind the Colonel in a line
and slogged across the flooded plains and bogs
   while aiming through the purpose of their minds.

Then Clark had noticed water deepening
   half way across the plain before the trees
and recognized that the canoes would need
   to help the soldiers who were weakening.

So the canoes were quickly sent ahead
   to drop the baggage when they found dry land
and then returned to help the weaker men
   so they would all arrive at the next camp.

At times the water rose to shoulder height
   and some men had to paddle through on logs
and all the men were pushing through the plight
   as they continued through the dogged slog.

Clark sent a group of men up in advance
   who were the strongest of the regiment
instructing them that when they reached dry land
   to holler out to give encouragement.

Then shouting out so all the men could hear
   with something tangible, confirmed and real,
they let the others know that land was near
   to bolster confidence with steadfast will.

Then Colonel Clark stood in the deepest part
   to guide the file that forded to dry ground,
emboldening the men to give them heart
   — they had to struggle on or they would drown.

On shore the men began to kindle fires
   as an enticement for the other troops
with light of warmth to further on their drive
   and lift the sinking spirits with a boost.

Some men were so exhausted at the shore
   they could not pull themselves out of the water
and had to wait until they had support
   with the assistance of the other soldiers.

The next day's travel was much easier
   by ferrying across a narrow lake
and the men's spirits were much merrier
   while marching in the sun on dry terrain.

Then from a stand of trees late in the day
   they saw the object of their long campaign
as they could see Vincennes 2 miles away
   across the open and uneven plain.

They also saw some men out hunting ducks
   and Clark sent Frenchmen who were with the group
to bring a villager back to the woods
   while hiding the main body of the troops.

Then speaking with the local villager
   Clark learned that they had many friends in town
and British fortified their garrison
   and had 500 soldiers by his count.

George Clark composed a message for the man
    to share with people living in the village
that with 1000 soldiers, his command
    would soon be marching to attack the British.

The people would be safe inside their homes,
    none of the soldiers would make an offense
but any villagers who were opposed
    should join the British troops and fight like men.

Clark had been careful to conceal his men,
    the British force was over twice their size
and fortified inside a garrison
    — to win this Colonel Clark had to be sly.

Then as Clark led his troops across the plain
    he marched and then he countermarched in ways
to use unevenness of the terrain
    to make it look like he had a brigade.

By night time they had gained the higher ground
    that overlooked the British at Vincennes
and Colonel Clark positioned next to town
    prepared to move upon the garrison.

Chapter 57

The Battle of Vincennes
February 23-24, 1779

Clark saw no sign the British were prepared
   — there were no pickets set outside of town.
He knew they either were caught unawares
   or posted to secure the garrison.

So Clark sent a lieutenant and some men
   to file through town that early evening
and fire upon the garrison's defense
   to stir the British fort's security.

Lieutenant Bailey then led 14 men
   into positions set around the fort
and when Clark saw the rifle fire begin
   he sent in more detachments for support.

George Clark was standing back so he could see
   any reactions from the garrison
to locate the defensive points of strength
   when British began firing in response.

Yet as the riflemen began to fire
   the garrison appeared to be asleep
and the offensive kept up for sometime
   before the British moved defensively.

It proved there often was town revelry
   when sudden spurts of gunfire would erupt
and in the fort the British took no heed
   until one of the soldiers had been struck.

A drum then sounded for a call to arms
    and then the garrison became alive
as musketry on battlements discharged
    and cannons from embrasures opened fire.

Then in the night Clark saw a clear outline
    of the defenses of the British fort
that was depicted with the flaring lights
    with every gun declaring a report.

The Patriots outside could move around
    and then take careful aim from place to place
but in the fort the British men were bound
    within the quarters of constricted space.

Then Colonel Clark led all the other men
    into the village with precise instructions
to keep a steady fire on the defense
    while giving the appearance of large numbers.

With 50 men set back for the reserve
    Clark had the officers announcing orders
so that their strident voices could be heard
    as if positioning large groups of soldiers.

The riflemen constructed some breastworks
    with railing from the fences and old boards
and were positioning close to the fort
    at distances no more than 30 yards.

The British cannons set in the blockhouse
    could not aim down and fired with no effect.
The riflemen were under the gun mounts
    that harmlessly discharged over their heads.

And when they opened the embrasure doors
　　the British blockhouse gunners were exposed
and the Kentucky riflemen would pour
　　the searing shot from flashing powder loads.

Then when the British muskets poked outside
　　from any loophole of the fort's defense
before the musket had a chance to fire
　　a dozen rifled balls went flying in.

Sometimes the Patriots would shout and taunt
　　in easy range of the artillery
then when the fort's embrasures opened up
　　the gunners were knocked out with riflery.

At dawn a small detachment had returned
　　with 20 British soldiers in the group
that had been out upon a scouting tour
　　and were completely lost for what to do.

But Clark could not send men out to attack.
　　The British might discover their small size
so messages were sent under truce flags
　　allowing for the group to go inside.

The group could not provide much reinforcement
　　and Clark could not leave British to his back.
Then when they were within the fort's defenses
　　he would have all the British soldiers trapped.

So Clark made sure that all the soldiers heard
　　to hold their fire upon the British force
and Clark made sure an open path was cleared
　　so the small group could scramble to the fort.

And ladders dropped allowing them to climb
    over the walls of the strong garrison
while Patriots were jeering the whole time
    as British thought Clark had 1000 men.

Then after all the British were inside
    the fight resumed soon after 9 AM
as riflemen kept up a steady fire
    to harry the surrounded British men.

Before nightfall a flag of truce appeared
    as Hamilton hoped to negotiate
and Colonel Clark sent terms that made it clear
    how Hamilton was to capitulate.

And there were some exchanges back and forth
    but Henry Hamilton was in a mess
while sieged by a large military force
    deep in the middle of the wilderness.

So the surrender of the fort was made
    and British soldiers left their stack of arms
then in the open they were all amazed
    — less than 200 soldiers were with Clark!

Clark captured a Lieutenant Governor,
    a garrison of British infantry
while gaining the control of a frontier
    with a Kentucky rifle company.

Chapter 58

John Paul Jones
October 23, 1779

A group of ships was led by John Paul Jones
    that cruised the cold and stormy northern seas,
patrolling boldly on the British coast
    in hunt of vessels from the Royal fleet.

Ben Franklin had arranged a ship from France
    to serve as squadron leader of the fleet
— the *Bonhomme Richard* under the command
    of John Paul Jones' naval mastery.

Then bearing south along Flamborough Head
    a large convoy was spotted miles away
and British flags were waving as they fled
    and John Paul Jones gave signal for the chase.

The merchant ships then huddled close to shore
    and John Paul Jones approached the 2 escorts,
one was a 20 cannon sloop of war
    the other was the frigate commodore.

A boat with Jones that hailed from France's fleet
    was signaled to engage the British sloop
and then the *Bonhomme Richard* turned to meet
    the ship *Serapis* — larger of the two.

The ship *Serapis* carried 50 guns
    — a British warship of the frigate class
with a displacement of expansive tons
    and cruised the sea with the square rigging masts.

The Royal ship gave battle dispositions
    and then the British signal gun was fired
and when the *Richard* came into position
    then Jones responded with a full broadside.

But after this initial volley shot
    the *Richard* struggled in maneuvering.
Serapis was a far more agile boat
    and kept evading Jones' strategies.

Then Jones steered straight into the British course
    to bring the ship athwart the British bow
and as the British tried to turn to port
    they caught the *Richard's* mizzen with their prow.

With the bowsprit caught on the mizzen mast
    the two boats swung together side by side
and Jones then grappled them together fast
    before *Serapis* loosened and slid by.

The sailors manned the swivels on top deck
    and raked the British ship above the boards
and muzzles of the heavy cannons pressed
    point blank upon each other ship's starboard.

Then John Paul Jones climbed to the lower deck
    to check the action of the gunning crews
but found the batteries were in a wreck
    as many of the heavy cannons blew.

The lower deck had 6 brass 18 pounders
    but some exploded the first shots they fired
and strewed the floor with dead and injured sailors
    and the whole battery was out of line.

Below the water line the ship was struck
    with solid shot that punched straight through the hull
and the boat's pumps were trying to keep up
    with water pouring through the gushing holes.

Then John Paul Jones climbed to the quarter deck
    with the 9 pounder cannon battery
and Jones was rallying the valiant men
    with only 2 of the guns servicing.

Then Jones instructed them to pull a gun
    that was positioned on the ship's lea side,
then John Paul Jones was helping to man one
    so they could service 3 guns the same time.

It was a brutal and horrific scene
    with British cannons firing at point blank
and muzzle flashes scorching oaken beams
    while shot was shattering the boards and planks.

The British yelled if Jones requested quarters
    as Jones was tamping down a solid 9
but John Paul Jones had not thought to surrender
    and yelled, "I have only begun to fight!"

Then Jones ignited the gun's powder charge
    and sent a solid shot into their boat.
The cannon bucked, recoiling back a yard
    and Jones then promptly started to reload.

The British 18 pounder battery
    was gutting out the *Richard's* lower deck
and British cannons fired incessantly
    as the two ships were locked and butting heads.

Jones ordered one 9 pounder to take aim
to topple the *Serapis'* main mast
and shattered boards began to catch with flames
as the two ships were burning with the blasts.

Then the main mast began to groan and shake
while shredded rigging dangled off the boat
and British officers feared it would break
and the ship's batteries began to slow.

The British commodore then struck the colors
and the fierce cannon fire came to a stop
as the *Serapis* then had been surrendered
and the poor *Richard* was victorious.

The fires on board had grown beyond control
and the remaining pumps could not keep up
with water pouring through the riddled hull
and the next day the *Bonhomme Richard* sunk.

Yet with the old converted cargo ship
and only 3 small cannons they could fire
Jones and his valiant crew of Patriots
captured a British warship for a prize.

1780

1780

Chapter 59

Charleston
January – May 1780

In Britain popular support had waned
  for fighting the colonial rebellion
with doubt for how the war could be sustained
  as the United States gained Independence.

One of the sparks igniting the conflict
  was stringent taxes on the colonies
to pay the debt for a long war with France
  and then the debt continued to increase.

Then war had been declared with France again
  and more alliances were being formed
as other nations had begun to stand
  opposed to British interests in the war.

So Henry Clinton built a strategy
  to redirect the war into the South
and then regain support with victories
  to ease the popular concerns and doubts.

The year before the British seized Savannah
  and Clinton sought a base of operations
and then decided on the town of Charleston
  as the headquarters for a new invasion.

But Charleston was a challenge for the British.
  Two previous attempts abjectly failed.
So this time Henry Clinton was determined
  the town would be completely overwhelmed.

George Washington remained outside New York
   and threatened British at the Hudson Bay
and Clinton left the body of his corps
   so 15,000 soldiers would remain.

Then General Clinton loaded up a fleet
   consisting of more than 100 ships
with horses and 8000 infantry
   and tons of stores so they would be equipped.

In February Clinton had made land
   within a tiny inlet south of Charleston
and soon his ranks grew to 10,000 men
   as Tories joined in General Clinton's army.

The Continental Army's General Lincoln
   commanded the defense of the port town
and the assembly bells in towns were ringing
   as word of the emergency spread round.

Ben Lincoln had a corps of Continentals
   — a force composed of 1500 men
and could call up 2000 from militias
   to garrison in town for a defense.

The 29th of March the siege began
   with lines of trenches and stout battlements
in machinations of the mass advance
   that built the pressure in slow increments.

Then after British built a solid line
   that could withstand a Patriot assault
they'd dispatch soldiers covered by the night
   to build additional advance redoubts.

Then in the morning Patriots would see
    a new position closer to the town
like heavy footsteps of colossal feet
    approaching on the open space of ground.

And Lincoln sent some sorties for attacks
    to try deterring British moving in
but had to carefully hold his men back
    to try retaining strength for the defense.

On April 8 some frigates made it past
    Fort Moultrie guarding entrance to the bay
to firmly tighten General Clinton's grasp
    to cut off all supplies and isolate.

The 13th British finished batteries
    within the range of Continental lines
and then the bombs of the artillery
    began to drop from arches through the sky.

The 19th British were 200 yards
    from the defenses of the Patriots
and cannons on each side were pounding hard
    with mortar bombs and solid iron shot.

The British had begun to bomb the town,
    the houses and the buildings were in range
and the alarms would regularly sound
    as parts of town were bursting into flames.

The night time was a spectacle to see
    with arches tracing through the open night
as burning fuses of the bombs would leave
    the paths of horror dropping from the sky.

Provisions in the town were nearly gone
   without a single shred of pork or beef
and the held stores of rice were nearly done
   with only tiny rations left to eat.

Then on the 8th of May the British set
   the army in position to advance
and General Clinton had a message sent
   for Lincoln to surrender the defense.

The British had by far the larger force
   and food in Charleston was in short supply
and there was no one near to lend support
   but Lincoln would not give without a fight.

When Clinton had received Lincoln's response
   the British launched a fiery cannonade
and bombs dropped on the town without a pause
   as buildings and the houses burst in flames.

Then Charleston's prominent civilian leaders
   met with the local Governor John Rutledge
and came to the decision to surrender
   and then arranged to speak with General Lincoln.

So Lincoln was pressed to capitulate
   to General Clinton without any terms.
He had no leverage to negotiate
   and Clinton took 5000 prisoners.

Chapter 60

Changing Command
June – August 1780

With Charleston as a military base
    for exercising a new strategy
then General Clinton furthered his campaign
    and issued on June 3 his policy.

— The people in America rebelled
    against King George's royal sovereignty
and they must work so the revolt was quelled
    and their compliance was compulsory.

They were required to actively suppress
    the opposition to the British reign
and fight against the insurrectionists
    to prove they were true subjects of the King.

This agitated local partisans
    and longtime neighbors became enemies
and factious groups became guerilla bands
    attacking one another ruthlessly.

Soon after General Clinton had rejoined
    his occupying army of New York
and left Cornwallis with the men deployed
    for the command of Charleston's southern port.

Cornwallis then began to set outposts
    into the Carolina countryside
extending his control in from the coast
    to keep the Patriots unorganized.

The Continental Army in the South
    was captured when the Patriots lost Charleston
and there were only scattered bands about
    that could coordinate an opposition.

The Continental Congress then decided
    for General Gates to lead the South's department
with his success at Saratoga sited
    as an assurance he could beat Cornwallis.

George Washington remained the chief command
    and held the British army in New York
and General Gates would muster up more men
    and then reform the Southern Patriots.

There was a single Continental camp
    — the last remaining in the Carolinas
at Hillsborough led by Johann de Kalb
    in a position right below Virginia.

The group consisted of 1000 men
    with light field pieces for artillery
— two Continental Army regiments
    and Colonel Armand's heavy cavalry.

The middle of the summer, late July,
    Gates had arrived and organized a march
although the soldiers lacked in their supplies
    and corn had not yet ripened at the farms.

There was a British outpost to the south
    — a distance of 180 miles,
that Gates was confident his force could trounce
    as Gates had plans to take them by surprise.

De Kalb suggested the march pause for food
    and veer by Charlotte to build up their stores
but Gates insisted they stay on the move
    before the outpost could be reinforced.

Along the march Gates gathered the militia
    that brought raw men and made the numbers swell
and totals of the soldiers topped 3000
    along with Colonels Stevens and Caswell.

Then 5 miles north of the outpost at Camden
    Gates issued orders for a night approach
but walking back to groups they were commanding
    the officers discussed what Gates had wrote.

Gates thought they had a force of 7000
    when they reported just 3000 men
and he was pressing in the forward column
    the raw recruits with no experience.

And Armand had been puzzled with the orders
    for cavalry to lead on a night march.
The picket posts would hear the noisy horses.
    They could not hide the clopping in the dark.

Gates ordered a big meal before attack
    with beef and then molasses on a mush
and cooks had breached what they thought were fresh casks
    and gave out ample servings to the troops.

It turned out victuals in the casks were spoiled
    and through the march the soldiers fell from ranks
discharging what they ate onto the soil
    and were too weak to fall back in again.

Then miles before they reached the edge of Camden
    they ran into the total British force
that had deployed with the exact same tactic
    to set up a surprise before the morn.

Then at midnight in the thick underbrush
    there was a pattering of musket fire
that was not able to build into much
    as all the soldiers fired completely blind.

It turned out Gates' plan was no surprise.
    The Tories warned the British days before
and soldiers with Cornwallis had arrived
    and Camden's outpost had been reinforced.

The two opposing lines had to draw back
    — no one could battle what no one could see
and tried to organize for an attack,
    impeded by the darkness, brush and trees.

Then Gates called for a council of command
    to hear the other officers' advice.
After a pause then Colonel Stevens said,
    "There's nothing left for us to do but fight."

Chapter 61

The Battle of Camden
August 16, 1780

All night the sound of scattered skirmishing
    announced the reconnoitering of lines
as they maneuvered in positioning
    for best advantage before morning light.

Gates set the Continentals to the right
    — the Maryland and Delaware brigades
with hardened veterans in sturdy files
    commanded by de Kalb in ordered ranks.

The center and the left were the militia
    composing over 2/3 of the corps
with raw recruits that lacked combat experience
    that steadies nerves of soldiers through the war.

At center were the Carolina men
    that mustered totals of 2000 strong
with Colonel Caswell leading the command
    as they were formed in battle lines at dawn.

At left with Colonel Edward Stevens stood
    Virginia volunteers who had marched down
with 700 soldiers for the troops
    to fight against the British further south.

The battle lines were formed by break of day
    and the command received intelligence
some British were 200 yards away
    at the front of Cornwallis' advance.

Then orders were sent with expedience
    as the redcoats were spotted in the breaks
and the first phase of battle was announced
    as the artillery began to play.

The adjutant then rode to the far back
    to tell Gates why the cannonade began,
describing dispositions of attack
    and the position of the line's defense.

The British were advancing on the left
    to gain advantage of the rough terrain
and were displaying marching regiments
    with an approach on Colonel Stevens' ranks.

Then after giving a clear explanation
    the adjutant expected a reply
from General Gates to order the engagement
    and counter the developing design.

But General Gates did not give a response
    and passively watched the developments
without initiating the command
    to actively maintain full ownership.

Instead of waiting for things to unfold
    then scramble to react to the events,
the General needed to take the control
    and not be subject to each circumstance.

The adjutant then clarified a point
    that if they stopped Cornwallis' first move
they could delay advances of his front
    so he could not position all his troops.

The adjutant said Stevens should move first
    to counter the advancing infantry
and hinder British so they could not form
    into a firing line defensively.

Then after an excruciating pause
    Gates grimaced and reluctantly agreed,
the adjutant then rushed to mount his horse,
    dispatching orders with an urgency.

And Otho Holland Williams later said
    this was the final order Gates then gave
as several times the adjutant had checked
    but for the whole day could not locate Gates.

The adjutant returned to Colonel Stevens
    with orders for his soldiers to advance
and then the adjutant made a suggestion
    and asked to borrow 50 of his men.

He planned to set a skirmish line ahead
    so British would make loose and careless shots
and spend their loads before the main force met
    for the advantage of the Patriots.

But by that time the British were well set.
    It was too late, they had formed battle lines
and charged on the small group with bayonets
    and scattered the raw soldiers by surprise.

As the men ran in panic toward the ranks
    a terrible contagion then caught hold
dissuading men from making a firm stand
    as they began to panic as a whole.

The soldiers did not wait to fire their guns,
   most had not seen the British infantry
and all the volunteers began to run
   — more from the fear than from hostility.

Then as the men ran to the center corps
   the other volunteers were stirred with fright
and suddenly 2/3 of the whole force
   were running off the field without a fight.

The Continentals on the right still stood
   and put up a fierce fight in bonded bands
and held the ranks with a tight brotherhood
   that only combat soldiers understand.

At times they even drove the British back
   although the British far outnumbered them
and fought off every organized attack
   with steady fire that cut down each offense.

They should have been withdrawn off of the field
   but Gates had never ordered a retreat
and one by one the veterans were killed
   while holding to the line courageously.

De Kalb was fighting fiercely on the ground
   and was inflicted with a mortal wound
and the proud veterans would not back down
   and boldly fought into the afternoon.

Cornwallis saw that the whole field was clear
   except for what remained of the brigades
and organized the British force to bear
   down on the group with a colossal wave.

With both the cavalry and infantry
    the British rushed with swords and bayonets
and charged with numbers overwhelmingly
    so the line broke with falling Patriots.

Gates had long since fled from the battlefield
    with no control or order for the men.
He dropped the sword he was assigned to wield
    and men dispersed the further on they fled.

Although Gates won a crucial victory
    at Saratoga in the north campaign
and captured Burgoyne and his infantry,
    he lost the Southern Army on this day.

Chapter 62

Benedict Arnold's Treason
September 25, 1780

At West Point on September 25
   George Washington and staff returned from Hartford
after communicating with the French
   about the site and the defense of Newport.

The fortress at West Point was a key site
   with stores and garrison and batteries,
the last defense upon the riverside
   to guard the waterway to Albany.

George Washington appointed General Arnold
   to take command of the important fort
as Arnold claimed he had not yet recovered
   from battle wounds he suffered in the war.

As General Arnold had made the request
   and with the services he had fulfilled,
the grant was made at Washington's behest
   in hopes that Arnold's wounds would quickly heal.

Then with the recent plans for a campaign
   the General offered Arnold his left wing
but Arnold said that he would rather stay
   and keep the fort that he was managing.

That day the General checked the residence
   but Arnold did not seem to be around.
Then Washington checked West Point's garrison
   and unexpectedly he was not found.

Then Washington accompanied with staff
    returned to Arnold's quarters set nearby
with questions of the absence of command
    when not one officer was notified.

Arnold had known that Washington had gone
    to hold a meeting at Connecticut
for the discussions as new plans were drawn
    to coordinate the French and Patriots.

There is no difference in a soldier's rank
    — when he has been assigned to hold a post
not privates nor the generals of brigades
    have leave without an authorizing note.

Soon after Colonel Jameson arrived
    and handed Washington an envelop
containing papers of the fort's design
    with counts of cannons, the supplies and troops.

The Colonel said militia soldiers caught
    a British spy who tried to sneak away
and found the package in his shoe and sock
    and brought him in where an arrest was made.

The British spy had tried to bribe the men
    with any sum of money they could name
but the poor soldiers valued the defense
    of their free Nation they would not betray.

The packet's letters were in Arnold's hand
    that General Washington could recognize
and other secret notes that were exchanged
    proved Arnold operated with the spy.

Arnold depleted West Point's garrison
    deliberately to compromise defense
and sabotage the Nation and the men
    from his own bitterness and selfishness.

Arnold ran in a panic hours before
    and scurried on one of the British fleet
— the royal ship, the *Vulture* sloop of war
    to pick the carcass of his dignity.

Arnold abandoned his own family,
    betrayed his Nation and his sacred oath
and proved devoid of the integrity
    that loyal soldiers honor and uphold.

Arnold made statements for his reasoning
    with specious, vacuous casuistry
but Arnold's choice was made in bitterness,
    forsaking honor for his vanity.

The soldiers then reformed the garrison
    to hold and man the cannons of the fort,
maintaining a strong national defense
    as General Washington secured West Point.

Chapter 63

British Advance in the Carolinas
August – October 1780

At Camden Gates' army was dispersed
   as soldiers scattered through the countryside,
providing a clear, undefended course,
   allowing British to extend their lines.

Cornwallis then advanced the British force
   that marched to overwhelm the town of Charlotte,
expanding their communications north
   while tying down their occupying collar.

Then with outposts established on roadways
   the British could communicate supplies
and infantry could rapidly convey
   to squelch and squash American designs.

So with the operation base at Charleston
   the British were extending out from town
and with a new position set in Charlotte
   Cornwallis certainly was gaining ground.

But in the mountains of the Carolinas
   the Patriots were managing strongholds
with raids conducted on the Brit's positions
   to complicate Cornwallis' control.

Cornwallis then dispatched a flanking column
   with the command of Major Ferguson,
to hold position closer to the mountains
   for the suppression of the Patriots.

Then Ferguson made Gilbert Town his base
    and with the help of local Tory groups
began attacking Patriot enclaves
    with British regulars and new recruits.

So Ferguson enforced a foreign power
    exerted over local residents
in the communities so to impoverish
    the independence of Americans.

The local leaders of communities
    were organizing the militia men
to fight against the British infantry
    to coordinate and battle Ferguson.

400 men were mustered in Virginia
    and led by William Campbell to the south
for the assistance of North Carolina
    to drive invasive British forces out.

And mountain men came down from Appalachia
    with John Sevier as well as Isaac Shelby
— 300 men from the frontier militias,
    sharpshooting riflemen now legendary.

Benjamin Cleveland and then Thomas Brandon
    and Edward Lacey along with James Williams
mustered 300 men and were soon marching
    in answer to the Patriotic calling.

When Tories had told Major Ferguson
    of local Patriots en route his way
he organized his men in Gilbert Town
    to form and urgently evacuate.

When Patriots converged at Gilbert Town
  the British force with Ferguson had left
and Patriots learned they were Charlotte bound
  to reach Cornwallis for protective help.

Then William Campbell ordered men with mounts
  to ride ahead and harry the rear guard
and force the troops retreating to turn round
  so Ferguson would have to stop the march.

Then when the British march was forced to stop
  the men on foot would soon be coming up
and they would all combine for an assault
  upon the isolated British troops.

The Patriots on foot had a forced march
  through a whole night and part of the next day
for nearly 50 miles through light and dark
  to block the British force from an escape.

Then Ferguson stood with 1000 men
  as Patriot militia were arriving
and British soldiers had a strong defense
  the 7th of October on King's Mountain.

Chapter 64

The Battle of King's Mountain
October 7, 1780

The Patriots assembled at King's Mountain
    and Campbell was appointed to command
so all the different groups that had assembled
    could coordinate to work in unison.

They managed holding Ferguson's retreat,
    before he reached Cornwallis' main force
but he had settled in defensively
    with a division of the British corps.

And Ferguson had gained a strong position
    upon the mountain's natural defense,
holding advantage of the elevation
    with tactical arrangements of his men.

Cornwallis would be sending reinforcements
    so Ferguson and his men could escape
and although Patriots were disadvantaged
    if Campbell waited it would be too late.

So Campbell ordered the assembled groups
    to form their companies around the mountain
and in position on that afternoon
    they'd hear the signal as his men were shouting.

Then as the Patriots rushed up the slopes
    the British could not pick a single side
to draw their infantry position's close
    for concentrations of their musket fire.

Then as the British were kept on the edge,
    they would advance with their sharpshooting skill
and then converge upon the mountain crest
    to topple Ferguson from top the hill.

The Patriots deployed in companies
    and after each position had been set
the Patriots began a hollering
    resounding through the hills with resonance.

The groups began to rapidly advance,
    adjusting to the oppositions met.
Some slopes were guarded with lines of defense.
    Others were open to the topmost ledge.

The group with Shelby met a guarding line
    positioned nearly halfway down the slope
but British ran after a searing fire
    then Shelby's marksmen tamped down a fresh load.

The other side ascended up the hill
    but were attacked by British bayonets
and Sevier's men stood boldly on the field
    and swung their guns like clubs in their defense.

The frontier men did not have bayonets
    and many of the soldiers were run through
and with the British line attacking them
    the men with Sevier cautiously withdrew.

Then as the British charge's surge was spent,
    before the British soldiers could reform,
Sevier had ordered up his riflemen
    who began tearing up the British force.

Then Shelby and some others had arrived
    upon the mountain from the other side
while driving back the British musket line
    as riflemen kept up a steady fire.

Each time the British organized a charge
    they'd rush with bayonets across the field
but then the riflemen picked them apart
    atop a new position on the hill.

At one point Ferguson deployed a Captain
    to march a company to patch a side
but in the transit riflemen attacked them
    and British fell before they reached the line.

Then Ferguson had British cavalry
    to form and make a charge upon their mounts
but climbing up into their stirruped seats
    the riflemen as quickly knocked them down.

James Williams' group then pressed on Ferguson
    who drove his horse to try to break the line
but then was felled by several rifle shots
    and Ferguson and Williams both lay dying.

The British waved white flags for their surrender,
    the battle had been won decisively
and with the capture of 800 soldiers
    the Patriots then cheered their victory.

As Williams lay, men stood attentively
    and let him know their triumph in the fight
and Williams said, "I die content since we
    have gained the victory." and then expired.

Cornwallis was informed of his great loss,
  as Patriots had captured a division
and forced the British Army to withdraw
  as they were then exposed in their position.

Without the column of their corps' left wing,
  the British line to Charlotte could be blocked
and posted at a distance from the sea
  Cornwallis' supplies would be cut off.

Cornwallis then evacuated Charlotte
  in a retreat close to an ocean port
and as he fell back to a post near Charleston
  he lost the leverage of his recent march.

1781

Chapter 65

Attack upon Virginia
January 1781

On New Year's Eve some ships cruised past the capes
    from the Atlantic to the Chesapeake
and the arriving 27 sails
    alarmed the people unexpectedly.

There were no notices sent from the north
    with warnings from the Continental Army
of British ships departing from New York
    where the main body of the fleet was mooring.

Two years before the British thrust assaults
    with a campaign into the Carolinas
and there were new concerns the British launched
    a plan for the invasion of Virginia.

American resources were stretched thin
    and soldiers suffered in dire misery
and a new wave of British coming in
    was threatening for a catastrophe.

The British were contained within New York
    and soldiers fought Cornwallis in the South
but then it seemed another British force
    had loaded up from England and sailed down.

George Washington was holding General Clinton
    with British forces and their naval fleet
but then there was a new threat in Virginia
    with transports loaded with more infantry.

On January 3 the British ships
   rode up James River on the rising tide
till a militia's battery defense
   sent solid shot into the vessels' sides.

A number of the British ships were struck
   as Patriot artillery was served
but with the damage no warships were sunk
   and British forces would not be deterred.

The ships began unloading infantry
   to storm the works and take the garrison
with numbers far beyond the battery
   consisting of no more than 50 men.

So the position was forced to withdraw
   after disrupting British with delays
and the militia from around was called
   for the defense of the United States.

The numbers mustered could not stop the fleet
   so they began to carry local stores
to places where they hoped to safely keep
   provisions and equipment for support.

The British marched into the town of Richmond
   and searched the homes and buildings for supplies
with the intent to make a strong impression
   then left the buildings and the homes on fire.

And in command of the marauding force
   was General Arnold whom the British King
had placed in charge of his own royal corps
   to prove his worth with brutal savagery.

Then Arnold yelled in bitter insolence,
  "Make sure you tell your chief George Washington
and also tell your Continental Congress
  that General Benedict Arnold did this!"

Chapter 66

The Weather of War
January 1781

After the shattering of Gates' army
    the delegates at Philadelphia
had to replace the head of the department
    and asked advice from General Washington.

Although he held the Army's chief command
    George Washington could not make the appointments,
one principle of the new government
    — the Generals were selected by the Congress.

George Washington proposed Nathanael Greene
    who proved to have a keen strategic sense
and with his tactical abilities
    he had excelled in general management.

An Army must stay operation ready
    and this requires the Army be maintained
with stern, strict drill and staple commissary
    ensuring a strong corps can be sustained.

The Armies are not where the wars are made.
    The wars result from failing politics.
The soldiers have enlisted to obey
    and to engage the threatening conflicts.

It has been proved through countless centuries
    as Virgil had poetically declared
— the only safeguard in preserving peace
    is vigilantly to prepare for war.

People are free to live on the bare ground
    and bear exposure to harsh elements
but any structure for a stable home
    must have the strength to withstand shifting winds.

So Congress had appointed General Greene
    to take command and lead the Southern Army
and organize the scattered infantry
    to fight against the army with Cornwallis.

Greene found most of the soldiers grouped in Charlotte
    and others gathered up in Hillsborough
as they were waiting for a General's orders
    for where to go and the next post to hold.

Cornwallis had retreated father south,
    reforming after Ferguson's defeat.
He'd lost a whole division in the rout
    and needed to repair depleted strength.

So as the Southern Army organized
    Nathanael Greene led the men on a march
to further press the Brit's retracted line
    and try to catch Cornwallis off his guard.

As they were marching in the winter time
    the Army strained supplies of local stores
so Greene had ordered the corps to divide
    to lighten the demands for their support.

The two divisions kept communications,
    so with a threat, they'd quickly recombine
while foraging in separate locations
    with close reconnaissance of British lines.

Greene led one group to the small town of Cheraw
    with modest winter stockpiles of provisions
and then the other led by Daniel Morgan
    marched farther west to post a new position.

On January 14 Morgan learned
    two different British groups were on the move
and watched to see which ways the groups would turn,
    observing what Cornwallis planned to do.

Dan Morgan camped along the Picolet
    with soldiers set next to the Grindales Ford
so they could use the river for defense
    by quickly crossing to the other shore.

But weather in a war is prone to change
    and water in the Picolet was high
with recent storms of heavy winter rain
    and British were no farther than 10 miles.

If Morgan tried to move his men across
    they could be caught while straddling the river
and could not form to fend off an assault
    and then he'd risk the loss of the division.

The British force was led by Colonel Tarleton
    and Morgan needed to change their location.
His men could not be backed up on the water
    so Morgan ordered the parade formations.

On January 16 Daniel Morgan
    had led a march 12 miles when he heard Tarleton
had reached their former camp along the river
    so Morgan set the battle lines at Cowpens.

Chapter 67

The Battle of Cowpens
January 17, 1781

That night Dan Morgan had his soldiers rest
    while sleeping on their arms in battle order,
removing the anticipated risks
    of an attack that night or early morning.

The men had shown their willingness to fight
    by joining in the country's military
and Morgan's leadership and wise design
    made sure the soldiers were well formed and ready.

The group consisted of some Continentals
    with mettle tempered with experience
but the distinctive regional militias
    composed more than 2/3 of all the men.

They would be facing British regulars
    with Colonel Tarletons's merciless dragoons.
The British would coordinate a charge
    the redcoats were well trained to execute.

Dan Morgan had selected sloping ground
    that favored the positioned Patriots
to have the upper hand while firing down
    as British infantry was marching up.

Morgan had seen how the militia spooked
    as previous engagements had collapsed
and told the men exactly what to do
    so raw recruits would not feel they were trapped.

The battlefield is an uncommon place
   where forces of extremity oppose
and only veterans can truly say
   how soldiers feel as marching ranks approach.

Dan Morgan formed the men into 3 lines
   to stagger the engagement of defense
with rifles in advance with skirmished fire
   to harry British soldiers marching in.

The 2nd line was formed of the militia
   with orders Morgan clearly emphasized
to fire their volleys in strong opposition
   then orderly withdraw to the left side.

Then Morgan ordered William Washington
   into position with the cavalry
to cover volunteers as they withdrew
   behind the Continental infantry.

Then the 3rd line commanded by John Howard
   consisted of the Continental men
combining with militia of Virginia
   to brace the final line of their defense.

The British force would suffer the two lines,
   first with the skirmishing of riflemen,
then the militias' volleyed walls of fire
   to send the British soldiers staggering.

Then the 3rd line would firmly hold the ground
   to stop advancing British on the hill
and as the first two lines had worn them down
   the Continentals would then clear the field.

An hour before the dawn horsemen arrived
    with news that Tarleton was 5 miles away,
then Patriots were drumming to their lines
    and set positions in assigned array.

At 7 in the morning on the field
    the British steadily were filing in
with practiced movements of parades and drill
    while broadly lining up the regiments.

And all the Patriots could clearly see
    as British formed into a battle line
— 1000 soldiers of their infantry
    with the dragoons positioned at each side.

The British formed 400 yards before
    the line of riflemen and skirmishers
and Tarleton seemed to have the larger force
    with a red wave of British regulars.

And Colonel Andrew Pickens rode the line
    with both instructions and encouragement
for the militias' timely volleyed fire
    they would coordinate by regiments.

And Pickens' clear instructions steadied them
    to wait until they heard the orders called
then thinning British ranks with volleys sent,
    the volunteers would orderly withdraw.

The British then were marching in advance
    and soon they saw the puffs of rifle smoke
and there were casualties of British men
    but steady ranks continued to approach.

The marksmen targeted the officers
  to throw the marching ranks into disorder
so uniformity would be disturbed
  as lines of their communications tore.

The riflemen were firing steady rounds
  but when the British closed 100 yards,
the redcoats began rushing cross the ground
  while yelling out in an impassioned charge.

The riflemen then rapidly drew back
  as officers emboldened volunteers
and joined them bracing for the next attack
  in the design of Morgan's 2nd tier.

It took a while for British to reform
  after their charge with bayonets was spent
and waited for their officers' report
  as their command was in dishevelment.

The riflemen had taken a sharp toll
  and the militia strengthened confidence
while watching British struggle to control
  the redcoat ranks that scrambled to reset.

The British then reformed and set a march
  but did not run into a skirmished fire
and soon realized they were in 50 yards
  of the American militia's line.

The volley fire tore through the British rows
  and sent the British soldiers reeling back
while thinning out the number of redcoats
  as the advancing British march was dashed.

Twice more the British formed for an advance.
  Twice more they met a line of musket fire.
Then as the British tried to form again
  the volunteers withdrew in ordered time.

When Tarleton saw the volunteers pull out
  he ordered his dragoons to make a charge
and rip the Patriots up in a rout
  while caught off guard in their withdrawing march.

The soldiers heard the thunder of the hooves
  that was approaching swiftly from behind
then Colonel Washington came rushing through
  and struck the British horsemen by surprise.

The dragoons thought they'd run straight through the files
  with slashing sabers hacking men apart
but lost their mounts while caught on the blind side
  as Washington led in a counter charge.

With the militia pulled off to the side
  the British then thought they could take the hill
and quickly formed into their battle line
  and made a rushing charge straight up the hill.

But as the British rushed atop the crest
  they reached another Patriot defense
with ordered ranks of the Virginia men
  lined up with soldiers of the Continent.

Colonel John Howard ordered them to fire
  and threw the regulars into disorder
and then the Patriots rushed in a line
  with bayonets to scatter British soldiers.

Then Morgan chased the British 20 miles
    and Tarleton lost his cannons and provisions
along with most the soldiers from his files
    and Charles Cornwallis lost one more division.

Chapter 68

Maneuvering Armies
January – March 1781

With General Morgan's victory at Cowpens
    Cornwallis and the British were enraged
and the main body of the British forces
    pursued Dan Morgan's Patriot brigades.

With myriad logistic challenges
    of coordinating armies on the move
Dan Morgan had 600 prisoners
    from the surrender of the British troops.

The Patriots were desperate for supplies
    upon forced marches on the muddy roads,
enduring the extremes of wintertime
    while battling both hunger and the cold.

But General Morgan could not take a break
    to let his hungry men forage for victuals.
They could not let Cornwallis overtake
    the gains the Patriots had earned in battle.

So every day the Patriots broke camp
    and set to march before the light of dawn,
outpacing Charles Cornwallis on their tracks,
    retaining the advantage they had won.

Then Morgan and his men reached the Catawba
    to ford the river on their passage north
and unexpectedly gained some good fortune
    as water rose soon after from a storm.

Then Morgan's men were marching to Virginia,
    ensuring that their gains were kept secure
while British were held at the flooded river
    until the water lowered at the fords.

By holding the large group of captive soldiers
    from joining with Cornwallis on the field,
it was another victory for Morgan
    without a single soldier being killed.

Then as Dan Morgan and his men escaped
    Nathanael Greene arrived at the Catawba
to guard the river's fording passageways
    and try to hold the British force from crossing.

Greene had militias post for 30 miles
    but when the water level slowly dropped
Cornwallis surged to force his soldiers by
    with weight of numbers that could not be stopped.

Then once Dan Morgan's soldiers were away
    Cornwallis turned his aim on General Greene
whose forces had been scattered and displaced
    to watch the fords that crossed Catawba's stream.

So General Greene began a slow withdrawal
    to gather the detachments of his men
and find a place a battle could be fought
    after he had reformed the Army's strength.

They travelled north and reached the Yadkin River
    and onerously forded cross their wagons
with long tow lines hauled by the hardy soldiers
    as wheels would bog beneath the burdened baggage.

And as the soldiers pulled supplies across
    they heard the riflemen's smart skirmishing
while holding back Cornwallis' front guard,
    reminding them of the dire urgency.

They did not have enough tents for the men.
    The ones they had kept stacks of muskets dry.
The men slept restlessly in rain and wind
    then marched all day for grueling miles and miles.

Cornwallis had destroyed his train of wagons
    in desperation to catch up with Greene
and Greene called in his officers for council
    for a discussion of their strategy.

The Patriots exhausted their provisions
    and Greene thought they should stop for an engagement
but all the council members were against this
    as numbers gave Cornwallis the advantage.

So Greene decided to continue north
    and recombine with General Morgan's men,
then bolstering the Continental force
    engage Cornwallis with a new offense.

Then General Greene sent out a fast detachment
    with Colonel "Light Horse" Lee and Colonel Howard
to slow Cornwallis in his forward action
    so the main body could catch up with Morgan.

Soon General Greene led the men to Virginia
    and then Cornwallis gave up on his chase
and Greene gained strength with regional militias
    while British had destroyed their wagon train.

With Lee and Howard harrying the British
  Cornwallis was outpaced in his pursuit
and could not follow Greene into Virginia
  without his wagons hauling gear and food.

Cornwallis then withdrew to Hillsborough,
  recruiting Tories to join British ranks
and Greene began to march back from the north
  and reached the Guilford Courthouse to make camp.

Chapter 69

The Battle of Guilford Courthouse
March 17, 1781

At Guilford Courthouse Greene set a defense
    with 3 lines toward Cornwallis' advance
just as Dan Morgan had set with success
    at Cowpens with his proven battle plan.

When General Greene approached toward Hillsborough
    after he had rebuilt the Army's strength,
he knew Marquis Cornwallis would deploy
    and set a march aggressively at him.

Cornwallis was determined to destroy
    the opposition in the Carolinas
to put the region in the King's control
    and pick apart the Nation's independence.

So on the road the British would approach
    Greene had the first row set behind a fence
with a broad musket line along their post
    to fire across the fallow openness.

Then after thinning out the British lines
    they would withdraw and join the 2nd front,
positioned in the standing woods behind
    and fire on British through the underbrush.

The 3rd line was positioned on a hill
    before the Guilford Courthouse seat of town
with Continental soldiers trained and drilled
    to hold their ranks and firmly stand their ground.

Greene had his horsemen watching out for miles
　　to guard against surprises at their flanks
and with thick forests through the countryside
　　Cornwallis had to follow the roadways.

On March 15 a message had confirmed
　　the British army was approaching fast
and Greene sent orders to his officers
　　so calls to arms were sounded with drum taps.

The camps were hopping as the soldiers raced
　　to grab their muskets for display of arms
and quickly fell into their files and ranks
　　then marched to posts to join the standing guards.

Positioned, all the soldiers had to wait
　　in eerie peace before a threatened fight
like friction building in a static state
　　before the flashing arcs of lightning strikes.

Across the broad, deep field the front line saw
　　Tarleton's dragoons arriving on the road
while reconnoitering in lead before
　　the massive British infantry's approach.

The British horsemen pointed at the fence
　　while grouping in discussion on their mounts
and recognizing the line of armed men
　　peered through field glasses to scope out the grounds.

Some horsemen turned and galloped back again
　　so that an urgent notice was dispatched
that they located the Americans
　　as British cavalry had made contact.

The Patriots were staring in the distance
    and could not hear the dragoons bandied fuss
but all the soldiers understood the business
    and knew they were the grist that was discussed.

At noon a river poured out on the field
    with redcoat columns marching in tight ranks
maneuvering like a colossal wheel
    that spanned the open to the farthest flanks.

The British soldiers tamped to load their guns
    in coordination of the regiments
then flashed and sparkled in the winter sun
    while fastening their deadly bayonets.

Then cross the field the rolling of the drums
    began to reach the ears of Patriots
as they all knew the march had then begun
    and every soldier checked his cartridge box.

The British splashed through Little Horsepen Creek
    and without stopping straightened out their line
and marched in unison in one broad sweep
    — a red and rising oceanic tide.

The sergeants steadied their positioned squads
    as focused officers were looking out
and soldiers clasped their guns in sweaty palms
    and they could feel their hearts begin to pound.

The order "Ready!" relayed down the line
    and soldiers rose and leveled out their aim
and sergeants spoke to urgently remind
    the men to steady and to mark the range.

The Patriots sent a well ordered volley
    and dozens of the British soldiers fell
but British infantry continued marching
    and without stopping their gaps were refilled.

The volley was sent at a longer range
    — the distance of 150 yards
then soldiers scrambled for their cartridges
    to quickly tamp down the next ball and charge.

Then when the British were at 50 yards
    the redcoat lines came to a sudden stop
and British soldiers lifted up their arms
    and sent a fiery blast of musket shot.

Few Patriots were able to reload
    and British charged with lowered bayonets
and the militia soldiers could not hold
    and fell back where the 2nd line was set.

With the next line set back into the woods
    the fighting carried on from tree to tree
and as the British tore into the bush
    the Patriots were fighting stubbornly.

Then after an extended bloody fight
    the 2nd line fell back to join the 3rd
across the field and up a sloping height
    and waited for the British to emerge.

After sometime the British formed their ranks
    at a clear distance of 500 yards
and then the tightly ordered regiments
    began the drumming of their cadenced march.

The Continentals formed the final line
   and stood in an unswerving steadiness
with tempered nerves to firmly hold their fire
   from drill, experience and discipline.

Then within 50 yards at a close range
   while looking British soldiers in the face
when their commander's orders had been made
   they blew the marching British line away.

The British ranks were thrown in disarray
   and soldiers staggered to the wooded edge
and Patriots thought they had won the day
   but then the British charged upon the left.

Then unexpectedly the left collapsed
   and British soldiers surged around the flank
and as the left wing began falling back
   their order started to disintegrate.

Then a battalion rallied and reformed
   and quickly launched into a counter charge
while Colonel Washington attacked with horse
   to fluster and confuse the British back.

And as the Patriots regained the ground
   while the two armies grappled in a fray
Marquis Cornwallis brought the cannons down
   and started firing canisters and grape.

Both British and Americans were struck
   as the artillery cut down the field
and General Greene gave orders to pull back
   before the valiant soldiers all were killed.

The British were too weary to pursue
   as Greene marched out the Army's infantry
and as the brave Americans withdrew
   Cornwallis had his Pyrrhic victory.

Chapter 70

Conditions of Development
March – April 1781

Greene camped the Patriots 10 miles away
    observing what Cornwallis planned to do
in battle disposition of the ranks
    if British forces launched in a pursuit.

Cornwallis stayed in Guilford for two days
    and tried to patch his damaged regiments
and buried soldiers in the shallow graves
    as trenches had been filled with wasted men.

Since Charles Cornwallis had destroyed his wagons
    he could not keep his army on the move.
They had no means to haul their gear and victuals
    that could sustain the marching of the troops.

So British forces slowly made retreat
    to Wilmington with access to the sea
and then made contact with the British fleet
    for shipments of supplies for their relief.

Greene trailed Cornwallis as his troops withdrew
    then turned the Patriots back toward the south
and left Marquis Cornwallis licking wounds
    and marched to clear the posts of British out.

Through the ensuing months the Patriots
    cleared British outposts set on the roadways
where the contentious partisans had fought
    as British tried invading Southern States.

And General Andrew Pickens led his group
    with General Francis "Swamp Fox" Marion
and Henry "Light Horse" Lee's swift mounted troops
    to clear out British posts and garrisons.

Cornwallis had then changed his strategy
    and turned his troops to march into Virginia
— the populous and fertile colony
    that was supplying General Greene's militia.

The Chesapeake could harbor fleets of ships
    and the deep rivers accessed far inland
so British forces could extend their grip
    and boat in the provisions for their camps.

Cornwallis could then cut off General Greene's
    communications with George Washington
and reassert the British monarchy
    from the position's central dominance.

On April 25 Cornwallis left
    the town of Wilmington nearby the coast,
informing Clinton of his change of step
    to march his redcoat army farther north.

As Clinton was still holding New York harbor
    he had been sending soldiers to Virginia
to reinforce marauding General Arnold
    and he approved Cornwallis' new mission.

George Washington had also sent an army
    under command of General Lafayette
and Lafayette's small forces had been marching
    to safeguard the Virginia Commonwealth.

And as the forces began their adjustments,
adapting to conditions as they changed,
they built another contest in the open
that was developing on a new stage.

Chapter 71

Management and Expedience
March – July 1781

The Army struggled with the short supplies
   which was a constant problem through the war
and punished the impoverished soldiers' lives
   in cold and hunger with the empty stores.

The Continental Congress worked to form
   a civil government that could sustain
the unity of states that had been born
   as independence was declared and gained.

The delegates confirmed the Articles
   of the Confederation of the States
but there were conflicts with particulars
   with obligations some refused to pay.

And General Washington wrote Governors
   explaining soldiers' dire necessities
in their important service in the war
   for the United States' security.

The soldiers from the states had not been paid
   with the arrears extending for a year.
The soldiers often did not eat for days
   and were without essential clothes and gear.

And Washington explained realities
   for the States' liberty to be preserved,
they must accept responsibilities
   and recognize the Nation's interests first.

The different States relied upon each other
   and if they compromised their unity
their whole endeavor would be torn asunder
   for independence and self-sovereignty.

The soldiers could not hold up the defense
   with famishes that hollowed out their strength
and there were no signs that the war would end
   without supplies to launch a strong offense.

The Northern Army set in Albany
   exhausted their provisions in their stores
and were beset with an emergency
   and stores were near exhaustion at West Point.

The Continental lines along New York
   were plagued with agitation and unrest
and shakily contained the British force
   with want of clothing and malnourishment.

And Washington could not dispatch supplies
   to help sustain Greene and the Southern troops,
the British in Virginia blocked the lines
   and all the Army had was lack of food.

In May more ships embarked from New York harbor
   with reinforcements sailing to Virginia
and General Clinton was depleting numbers
   while building up Cornwallis' position.

This opened a new opportunity
   that General Washington could clearly see
with General Clinton's forces weakening
   by him deploying British infantry.

Then Washington discussed with Rochambeau
    who held the French position at Newport
to coordinate, attack and overthrow
    the British force that occupied New York.

In June Cornwallis had 6000 men
    with infantry arriving from New York
and he attacked the town of Charlottesville
    and burned supplies stored at the Point of Forks.

And Lafayette was held to skirmishing
    without the strength for a direct offense
and deftly managed rifle companies
    to keep Cornwallis turning in defense.

Attacking New York would give some relief
    so Lafayette could muster more militia
and Clinton could not reach the Chesapeake
    to strengthen British forces in Virginia.

Then Washington heard news from General Greene
    — the Southern Army had reclaimed Augusta
and drove the British forces to the sea
    where they were held in Charleston and Savannah.

July the French and Patriots had formed
    with Rochambeau and General Washington,
positioning their columns at New York
    to launch attacks on British battlements.

Then Rochambeau and Washington received
    a message from the French West Indies fleet
— de Grasse was sailing to the Chesapeake
    with warships and 3000 infantry.

That instant Washington could see the end,
　　not just for an advantage, but far more
and Rochambeau and he prepared to send
　　the Armies marching south to end the war.

Chapter 72

The March to Yorktown
August – September 1781

Although the situation offered promise
    there was no guarantee for a success
and Washington had to convey two Armies
    450 miles in rapidness.

George Washington then staged a demonstration
    to concentrate at a New Jersey camp
preparing an assault on Staten Island
    to capture British at their garrison.

Then both the French and the Americans
    could move across the state without alarm
and Clinton would be manning battlements
    without suspecting the intended march.

And as they ferried cross the Hudson River
    and marched along New Jersey to the south
the allied Armies would appear intending
    to reach the camp around Eliz'bethtown.

George Washington instructed Lafayette
    to hold Marquis Cornwallis in his place,
the marching Army of the Continent
    along with Rochambeau were on the way.

Then news Cornwallis moved into Yorktown
    and had been digging in with battlements
meant he would not attempt escaping south
    to Charleston or Savannah garrisons.

The British knew de Grasse was sailing north
    but thought his destination was New York
as Clinton was observing from the port
    George Washington positioning his force.

So General Clinton had the British fleet
    weigh anchor and sail from the Chesapeake
to guard the Hudson Bay defensively
    as Clinton was expecting to be sieged.

Then with the grand theatrics of the camp
    where the Americans and French amassed
they looked like they were staging an attack
    while they were waiting to hear from de Grasse.

Then Washington deployed the regiments
    that marched to Princeton farther to the south,
then Trenton, Philadelphia again
    through those old battlefields to reach Yorktown.

The time the British fleet had reached New York
    and blocked the Hudson Bay from the French fleet
the allied Armies had set a new course
    with a surprising change of strategy.

The British ships had left the Chesapeake
    and quickly set into a new position
then at Virginia France's naval fleet
    made a safe harbor without opposition.

The allied Armies were stretched out for miles,
    Marquis Cornwallis and his men were caught.
And Patriots rolled drums and played the fifes
    to a decisive battle to be fought.

3000 soldiers landed with de Grasse
    and reinforced Marquis de Lafayette
and Patriots continued on their march
    along with Rochambeau and more Frenchmen.

September 5 the British fleet returned,
    de Grasse engaged them in the open sea
and Britain's mariner command was turned
    with Comte de Grasse's naval victory.

And with the British maritime defeat,
    de Grasse's warships harbored in the bay,
commanding waters of the Chesapeake
    to block Marquis Cornwallis from escape.

The long lines of the Armies soon arrived
    — platoons and companies and regiments,
battalions and brigades of ranks and files
    with drums and fifes of military men.

They organized in an expansive camp
    where Lafayette was set at Williamsburg
and with George Washington in the command
    they were prepared for a decisive turn.

September 28 the camp broke down
    and soldiers marched a glorious parade
to siege the Brits surrounded at Yorktown
    with the French fleet positioned in the bay.

Chapter 73

Tightening the Vise
October 5-9, 1781

The allied Armies camped around Yorktown
    with Patriots at right and France at left
and British forces were completely bound
    as the enclosure of the siege was set.

And the commanders kept a high alarm
    to guard against a counter, sortie strike
and all the soldiers slept upon their arms
    prepared to man the lines at any time.

And as they brought the stores and heavy guns
    they were prepared to press the massive weight
and plans for tighter works had then begun
    to set artillery in firing range.

But setting down a more constrictive line
    to push and pressure British battlements
exposed the soldiers to the British fire
    while toiling dutifully to dig each trench.

So a new parallel that had been planned
    required a careful, coordinated start
to quickly set up a secure defense
    under the secret cover of the dark.

2000 soldiers in a single night
    would wield the picks and shovels, not their arms,
to dig the works of the entrenchment line
    with British posts within 200 yards.

October 5 after the sun had set
   the officers marked out the plan's design
and listening for orders to begin
   the soldiers waited where they were assigned.

One sergeant waited with his sapper squad
   — Joseph Plumb Martin of Connecticut
who joined the Army when he was 15,
   6 years before when the war had begun.

And in the dark a gentleman approached
   to ask where he could find the officers
and Martin and the man politely spoke
   in cautionary care of quiet words.

The man was told the officers were found
   and parted with a thoughtful courtesy
and Martin was surprised by the faint sound
   when officers said, "Your Excellency."

Then Martin realized with whom he had spoke
   and paused a moment in astonishment
through the entire exchange he did not know
   the gentleman was General Washington.

The soldiers then set to their earnest work
   and dug all night to excavate a trench
while trying quietly not to disturb
   the bulldogs sleeping nearby in the pens.

By morning they had laid out the advance
   with segments that had been marked on the ground
meeting complete in a continuance
   encircling the British in Yorktown.

At the first light the British had realized
    the closing line of French and Patriots
but by the time their cannons opened fire
    the soldiers were secure behind breastworks.

For days the allies built the batteries
    and were positioning artillery
and set the heavy guns methodically
    to tighten down the vises of the siege.

They rolled in cannons, mortars, howitzers
    and totaled up the 92 big guns
with stores of shot and bombs and canisters
    laboriously hauled in by the tons.

October 9 the batteries were done
    and with their expertise and discipline
the veterans were standing by their guns
    while waiting for the signal to begin.

The Patriot commanding battery
    had 10 big guns in front of the flagstaff
and everyone was waiting patiently
    to see the signal raised upon the mast.

Then at high noon the flag began to rise
    and lifted up the soldiers with the sight
through honor, courage and their duty's pride
    with glory of the waving Stars and Stripes.

Then with the signal all the cannons fired
    in a salute that sent out solid shot
with cannonades upon the British line
    and once commenced the firing did not stop.

Chapter 74

Removing All Doubt
October 11-16, 1781

October the 11th regiments
    had then begun a 2nd parallel
and tightened hold in steady increments
    while pounding British lines with shot and shell.

Before they could complete the battlements
    and dig the trenches to the riverside
two British redoubts were set in advance
    before the main works of the British line.

The redoubts blocked the 2nd parallel
    from the construction's purpose as a whole.
If incomplete the siege was doomed to fail
    and with a gap the line would never hold.

Then early in the night on the 14th
    detachments formed to charge the 2 redoubts
and overwhelmed the forts with lightning speed
    then quickly turned the British cannons round.

They finished the entrenchments on that night
    and as the captured cannons turned about
they had completely closed the siege's line
    with the inclusion of the seized redoubts.

Then the artillery was brought up front
    and set before the British at close range
with repositioning of the big guns
    advancing the siege to the final stage.

For days the allied cannons fired away
    and pounded on the British battlements
with cannonades throughout the night and day
    as the bombardment was continuous.

They aimed the heavy guns at the embrasures
    and knocked the British cannons off their mounts
and silenced opposition in good measure
    as redcoat batteries were pummeled down.

Three British transports and a frigate burned
    after receiving red hot cannon shot
and the explosion shook the very earth
    when powder in the frigate hold had caught.

October 16 redcoats launched a sortie
    and spiked the cannons of a battery
but quickly scrambled back before the morning
    with Continentals rushing in relief.

The Patriots then reinforced their guards.
    It was no time for allies to relax.
They had pinned down Cornwallis' whole corps.
    They had to keep on pressing the attack.

Chapter 75

Victory
October 17, 1781

The cannonade kept pounding through the night
  and on the morning of the 17th
the shot continued hammering the lines
  with thundering of the artillery.

At 10 that morning Ebenezer Denny,
  an officer from Pennsylvania,
was watching with the others in the Army
  for movements from the British battlements.

Then Denny saw upon one parapet
  a single man in British uniform
stood with his drum and wooden drumming sticks
  directly in the cannonading storm.

The British soldier's drum could not be heard,
  the roaring of the cannons was too loud
and officers began to shout the word
  for all the cannon gunners to stand-down.

Then one by one the batteries ceased fire
  and the thick clouds of smoke began to clear
and the one drummer sounded out the time
  as if the whole wide world had hushed to hear.

A British officer then joined the drummer
  and after pulling out his handkerchief
waved it for the announcement of surrender
  and the United States cheered "Victory!"

1782

&

1783

Chapter 76

Independence

The next year of the 18th Century,
    the British House of Commons had a vote
demanding end of the hostilities
    although King George defiantly opposed.

In April the new Ministry met Franklin
    for a discussion set in Paris, France
with an exchange for peace negotiations
    in hope to bring the conflict to an end.

As the discussions were then underway
    the British forces paused from their attacks
but inside Charleston and the Hudson Bay
    the British garrisons remained intact.

In May George Washington received a letter
    from Colonel Nicola in secrecy,
declaring Washington become dictator
    that Washington denounced vehemently.

They had been fighting through a brutal war
    to free the People from a tyranny.
He would not let oppression be restored
    when they were on the verge of liberty.

George Washington opposed the special interests
    whether his own or any other region.
They fought for liberty to share together
    and serve the greatest interest of the Nation.

The next year General Washington then learned
    of plans of some insurgent officers
incited by anonymous brochures
    that would dishonor all they had fought for.

The soldiers were upset with the arrears
    and disregard of sacrifices made.
They suffered terribly throughout the war
    and all they gave was being cast away.

Then Washington spoke to the officers
    of duty and the honor they had earned
so wild emotions did not overturn
    the principles and reasons they had served.

And after Washington spoke to the men
    who gathered at the meeting at Newburgh,
the officers lined up to Washington
    profoundly moved by what they all had heard.

September a peace treaty had been signed
    and British ships were leaving from the ports
and Washington rode with the ranks and files
    to lead the Army back into New York.

Then gathering December 23
    in ceremony at Annapolis
George Washington retired his polished sword
    to join again the private populace.

Epilogue

Epilogue

Epilogue

The gaining of the Nation's independence
  with sovereignty of the United States
essentially was only the beginning
  for gracious liberty to be sustained.

Fulfilling a full course of revolution,
  after the settled peace had been achieved,
the Founders ratified the Constitution
  securing common rights and liberty.

After the war George Washington's ambition
  was to reside in quiet, private life.
Once the United States gained independence
  his longing was to peacefully retire.

But with insistence of the Congressmen
  to steady the established government,
he served 2 terms as the 1st President
  with the approval of the populace.

Then Washington's upright integrity
  led him to be an abolitionist
electing to give his slaves liberty
  which was his final will and testament.

And through the Founder's courage, strength and vision
  they opened liberty through independence,
then formed the Constitution of the Nation
  and gave this gift completely to The People.

Acknowledgements

But poets read history to collect the flowers not fruits — they
attend the fanciful images, not the effects of social institutions.
— John Adams

However John Adams' statement may apply to my poem's
portrayal of the American Revolution, with the insights of his
writing and the writings of other Founders, I have attempted to
explain the substance as well as evoke the spirit in the War for
Independence.

This poem is based upon the first person accounts of historic
figures, most of which are found in the volumes of the Library of
America. In as many instances as possible, the figures appear in
the poem as my poetic narrative was composed from the
perspective of looking over their shoulders through the depictions
of their accounts.

Additionally, Craig L. Symonds' *A Battlefield Atlas of the
American Revolution* was invaluable in providing concise
explanations of operational and battlefield logistics. I also
consulted Michael Stephenson's *Patriot Battles* for technical
information about the equipment used during the period.

My aspiration in the composition of *Liberty Bell* was to
acknowledge the precious gift of liberty and increase the respect
and appreciation for the vision, courage and self-sacrifice of the
Founders of the United States of America. They won
independence, developed the Constitution for the Federal Republic
of the United States of America to protect the liberty provided
through this independence and then selflessly gave this gift to the
People. This gift can only be preserved through the daily diligence
of the People.

Garrett Buhl Robinson

Bibliography

Primary Sources

Adams, John. *Revolutionary Writings 1755-1775*, edited by Gordon S. Wood, New York: Literary Classics of the United States, 2011. Library of America #213.

Adams, John. *Revolutionary Writings 1775-1783*, edited by Gordon S. Wood, New York: Literary Classics of the United States, 2011. Library of America #214.

Adams, Abigail. *Letters*, edited by Edith Gelles, New York: Literary Classics of the United States, 2016. Library of America #275

Addison, Joseph. *Cato: A Tragedy, and Selected Essays*, edited by Christine Dunn Henderson and Mark E. Yellin, Indianapolis, Indiana: Liberty Fund, 2004.

Franklin, Benjamin. *Silence Dogood, The Busy-Body, and Early Writings*, edited by J. A. Leo Lemay, New York: Literary Classics of the United States, 2005. Library of America #37A.

Franklin, Benjamin. *Autobiography, Poor Richard & Later Writings*, edited by J. A. Leo Lemay, New York: Literary Classics of the United States, 2005. Library of America #37B.

Hamilton, Alexander. *Writings*, edited by Joanne B. Freeman, New York: Literary Classics of the United States, 2001. Library of America #129.

Jefferson, Thomas. *Writings*, edited by Merrill D. Peterson, New York: Literary Classics of the United States, 1984. Library of America #17.

Locke, John. *Second Treatise of Government*, edited by C. B. Macpherson, Indianapolis, Indiana: Hackett Publishing Company, Inc., 1980.

Marshall, John. *Writings*, edited by Charles F. Hobson, New York: Literary Classics of the United States, 2010. Library of America #198.

Martin, Joseph Plumb. *A Narrative of a Revolutionary Soldier*, New York: Signet Classics, 2001.

Paine, Thomas. *Collected Writings*, edited by Eric Foner, New York: Literary Classics of the United States, 1995. Library of America #76.

The American Revolution: Writings from the War of Independence 1775-1783, edited by John Rhodehamel, New York: Literary Classics of the United States, 2001. Library of America #123.

The American Revolution, Writings from the Pamphlet Debate 1764-1772, edited by Gordon S. Wood, New York: Literary Classics of the United States, 2015. Library of America #265.

The American Revolution, Writings from the Pamphlet Debate 1773-1776, edited by Gordon S. Wood, New York: Literary Classics of the United States, 2015. Library of America #266.

Washington, George. *Writings.* edited by John Rhodehamel, New York: Literary Classics of the United States, 1997. Library of America #91.

Secondary Sources

Brown, Richard H. and Cohen, Paul E. *Revolution: Mapping the Road to American Independence*, New York: W. W. Norton & Company, 2015.

Gross, Robert A. *The Minutemen and Their World, Revised and Expanded Edition*, New York: Picador, 2022.

McDowell, Bart. *The Revolutionary War*, Washington, D.C.: The National Geographic Society, 1967.

Ricks, Thomas E. *First Principles*, New York: Harper Collins, 2020

Stephenson, Michael. *Patriot Battles*, New York: Harper Perennial, 2008.

Symonds, Craig L. *A Battlefield Atlas of the American Revolution*, California: Savas Beatie, 2018.

The Founding Fathers, Hoboken, New Jersey: John Wiley & Sons, 2007.

Whitman, Walt. *Poetry and Prose*, edited by Justin Kaplan, New York: Literary Classics of the United States, 1982. Library of America #3

Index

Also by Garrett Buhl Robinson

Poetry
Pilgrims
Ballet Lessons
Songs for Walt
Whispering Emily
Satires
Little Pieces of Poetry
City of Poems
The Ballad of Emperor Norton
A Man Who Lives in a Dream
The Nobody
Beauty beyond Reason
Martha, a poem

Fiction
Zoë
Nunatak

Theater
Letters to Zoey
The Nobody

Poet in the Park®
In Humanity I see Grace, Beauty and Dignity.
PoetinthePark.com

www.ingramcontent.com/pod-product-compliance
Lightning Source LLC
Chambersburg PA
CBHW020431130626
46549CB00001B/91